I0791192

THE DESTINY OF HUMANITY

VIEWS GLEANED FROM THE SCIENTIFIC PRINCIPLES OF NATURE

L Zhang, Ph.D.

Archway Publishing books may be ordered through booksellers or by contacting:

Archway Publishing
1663 Liberty Drive
Bloomington, IN 47403
www.archwaypublishing.com
844-669-3957

ISBN: 978-1-6657-2638-2 (sc)
ISBN: 978-1-6657-2639-9 (e)
Library of Congress Control Number: 2022912330

Print information available on the last page.

Archway Publishing rev. date: 07/08/2022

ACKNOWLEDGEMENTS

I deeply appreciate the caring and support from my loving parents and those teachers from primary school to college who cared about me and wished me to do better than them. Their love and caring motivated me daily to overcome obstacles and challenges in my life and career. I also thank my close family members for their love and support during the past decades. Without their support, I would not have been able to accomplish what I have in my career.

PREFACE

The Destiny of Humanity aims to bridge the gap between modern science and technology and the spiritual values of human societies. In recent years, humanity has experienced dramatic advances in medicine, science, and technology. Yet, humanity is facing unprecedented challenges: deadly conflicts arising between different groups and societies, major disasters frequently occurring all over the world, constant threats of pandemic and epidemic … Importantly, the modern human experience has demonstrated the awesome power of scientific principles: to dramatically improve health and extend lifespan; to create the internet, powerful computers, mobile devices, and robots that fundamentally change the ways of human living; and to build weapons of mass destruction. It is therefore worth exploring the idea that these scientific principles may also help humanity to overcome these unprecedented challenges facing humanity today.

The Destiny of Humanity analyzes major scientific principles of chemistry, biology, physics, and statistics, to reveal their relevance to human traits, the interaction between humans and nature, and the interaction among humans. It crystallizes a unifying moral compass that is compatible with advanced science and technology and can guide the application of powerful emerging technologies. This book is unified and logical in presentation. It is written in such a way that curious readers with a preliminary understanding of science can comprehend the scientific principles and their relevance to human societies. This book aims to elicit a new way of thinking about the future of humanity and how to tackle the grave challenges facing humanity.

CONTENTS

INTRODUCTION

Despite the tremendous advances in science and technology in the new millennium, humanity faces unprecedented challenges on several fronts. These challenges are related to the interactions between humans and nature, humans and humans, and society and society. With regard to nature, the mass extinction of biological species caused by human overpopulation, pollution, and environmental changes pose a serious threat to the long-term survival and development of humanity. With regard to humans and societies, major threats stem from the lack of a universal moral compass, causing conflicts among different cultures, religions, communities, and political groups within one country, like the USA. This threat has existed since the Common Era but is now exacerbated and magnified by advanced technologies. Another major threat results from the advancement of science and technology, particularly in the area of biotechnology and artificial intelligence.

The fundamental cause for these tremendous challenges and threats is the lack of a universal moral compass that is able to guide the development and application of powerful technologies. Currently dominant religious doctrines and theories originated prior to the new millennium—a new era when previously unimaginable and unprecedented breakthroughs in physical, chemical, biological, and computational sciences and technologies have emerged. The currently dominant belief systems in leading Western societies have their roots in religious doctrines that were formulated when humans believed that Earth was the center of the universe, and the human population was only about 2.5 percent of today's population. These doctrines are highly incompatible with modernity and cannot serve to properly guide the application of advanced science and technology and the development of humanity, with 7.9 billion humans and an increasing population on Earth. There is an incompatibility of these belief systems with modern science and technology. The conflict between dominant human belief systems and the potential destructive power afforded by modern science and technology poses a grave threat to the survival and development of humanity in the not-too-distant future.

This book aims to provide a scientific and logical basis for formulating a unifying ethical and moral compass that is compatible with the advanced science and technology of the new millennium. This book will review and apply relevant scientific principles from natural sciences, including physics, chemistry, biology, and statistics, to analyze and compare human interactions with analogous interactions in nature in order to understand, predict, and guide humanity. Chapter 1 considers chemical bonding between atoms and compares the characteristics of chemical bonding with those of human bonding. The analogy between chemical bonding and human bonding exists at multiple levels and is remarkable.

Chapter 2 first reviews the solubility principles when different chemical compounds are mixed and the factors that can alter solubility. Comparable factors will then be identified and applied to the mixing and interacting of humans, different cultures, and communities to highlight the conditions and factors that influence intercultural interactions.

Chapter 3 discusses biological diversity and the associated genetic variations. It is fascinating how diverse living organisms are on Earth, how much genetic variation exists, and that such variation is beneficial to the survival of living organisms. Chapter 4 reviews normal distribution and how it is applied to describe the variations in errors of measurements in astronomical observations and in the variations of human traits called quantitative traits. Most physical and mental traits are quantitative. How the distribution of human traits influences the governance principles of human societies is considered.

Chapter 5 examines nuclear reactions and their characteristics and how the information may be relevant to the development of humanity. Chapter 6 analyzes the major threats to the survival and development of humanity in an era with rapidly advancing technologies that dramatically alter the interactions of humans, communities, and countries. The underlying factors of these threats are considered. Finally, Chapter 7 synthesizes relevant facts and scientific principles discussed in chapters 1 to 5 and reveals a universal moral and ethical compass that enables the healthy development of humanity and human diversity at many levels, including the diversity of individuals, communities, and countries.

This book intends to provoke serious thoughts and

considerations about modern human societies and the importance of a moral compass that is compatible with the scientific principles that underlie the advanced biological, nuclear, and computational technologies. The environment on Earth is clearly deteriorating, likely due to a range of factors including human overpopulation and climate change. Thus, there are a lot of emotional outcries and calls to action from various segments of society, ranging from politicians to the public. However, these calls are often based on untested hypotheses, not on confirmed facts. What is lacking is solid data that provide convincing proof for the effectiveness of some popular policy actions. Solutions are not considered along with other crucial factors, such as the size of the human population and highly unequal living conditions in different parts of the world. Certain policies are driven by emerging businesses to make profits. There is a universal lack of rational and in-depth consideration of multiple confounding factors by governments and interest groups.

When it concerns the future of Earth and humanity, it is necessary to consider all crucial factors and come up with logically and scientifically sound steps forward without the rush to benefit a new class of businesses. Despite the advanced technologies, a good portion of humans in the world still live under very poor conditions. The ideological and materialistic conflicts among communities, cultures, and countries are as great as ever, and the impact of such conflicts is exacerbated by advanced technologies. Thus, it is worthwhile to explore potential new ways of thinking and acting that may guide humanity to a better future and to avoid catastrophic consequences. This book aims to elicit such thinking.

1

FROM CHEMICAL BONDING
TO HUMAN BONDING

Currently, there are 118 recognized chemical elements in the periodic table. However, most substances on Earth are not elements; they are compounds. Chemical compounds are substances composed of identical molecules consisting of atoms from more than one element. They are made up of a combination of elements in a fixed ratio. A compound often does not act like the elements that make it up. For example, salt is sodium chloride, but it does not act like sodium or chloride. This is because after sodium and chloride are joined together by a chemical bond, the compound exhibits completely different properties. A chemical bond is a force that holds atoms of elements together in compounds. These bonds, chemical forces, can allow the formation of countless new compounds by combining elements in various ways.

The human body contains countless atoms. The size of atoms is in angstroms ($Å$; 10^{-10} meter), with a diameter ranging from about 1–5 $Å$. The human body size is ten billion times that of atoms. It would seem utterly ridiculous to think that we could learn anything from the behaviors of simple atoms to enlighten our understanding of complex humans. Yet if we allow ourselves to conceptually extract the essence of atom interactions/bonding and compare it with human interactions/bonding, we may see that there are amazing similarities and analogous modes.

Why do we compare human bonding with the bonding of atoms, i.e., chemical bonding, and not bonding between electrons or other particles like neutrons? The answer is that there are many analogies between chemical bonding and human bonding in their complexity and modes. To reveal these analogous modes, we first consider chemical bonding between atoms. Types of chemical bonds include the strong bonds (i.e., ionic and covalent bonds), the metallic bond, and weak secondary forces, such as the hydrogen bond and the van der Waals force. An ionic bond is formed by transfer of electron(s) from one atom to another, and positively and negatively charged ions are held together by electrostatic forces, such as the bond in Na^+Cl^-. Those atoms that have lost electrons obtain a net positive charge and are called cations. Those atoms that have gained electrons obtain a net negative charge and are called anions. The relative strength of an ionic bond increases with the charges of ions and decreases with the distance between two ions. Ionic compounds often form crystals and have high melting and boiling points.

A covalent bond is formed by the sharing of one or more pairs of electrons with opposite spin between two atoms. The valence bond theory assumes that covalent bonds are formed when atomic orbitals overlap, and that the strength of a covalent bond is proportional to the amount of overlap. Thus, covalent bond formation does not require oppositely charged atoms and can be formed with the same atom, such as in the oxygen molecule (O_2) and nitrogen molecule (N_2) and between different atoms, such in CH_4 and CO. The simplest example of a covalent bond is formed when two hydrogen atoms come together to form a hydrogen molecule, H_2. This bond is 100 percent covalent. Covalent compounds often have low melting and boiling points and cannot conduct electricity. Most bonds are not 100 percent ionic or 100 percent covalent. There is often covalence in ionic bonds and ionicity in covalent bonds. Ionic and covalent bonds are strong.

There are weak bonds that are formed between the atoms of different molecules. The hydrogen bond is formed when a hydrogen bonded with one electron-rich atom also interacts with another electron-rich atom. Hydrogen bonding is a special type of dipole-dipole attraction. Hydrogen bonds are weaker than covalent or ionic bonds but are generally stronger than ordinary dipole-dipole interactions and dispersion forces. Van der Waals force is the weak force between permanent molecular dipoles, between permanent dipoles and induced dipoles, and between instantaneously induced dipoles. The London dispersion force is a temporary attractive force resulting from an induced dipole-dipole attraction when electrons from two adjacent atoms occupy positions that make them form temporary dipoles.

While strong bonds allow atoms to form molecules, the weak bonds affect the group properties of the molecules, such as liquefaction, solidification, and solubility. Weak bonds are particularly important in large biological molecules for stabilizing their structures and shapes. Hydrogen bonds stabilize the structures of DNA (deoxyribonucleic acid), RNA (ribonucleic acid), and proteins, the building blocks of life. Hydrogen bonds also provide many crucial, life-sustaining properties of water.

It is worth noting that human bonding is analogous to chemical bonding in many aspects. The strong human bonds are those formed by close family members or partners. One kind is the bond formed by sexual attraction, which may be considered analogous to ionic bond. Another kind of strong bond is those formed by siblings, between parents and children, between people with shared values and beliefs. This would be analogous to covalent bond. Construction of families can also be quite analogous to the construction of molecules: from simple, like CO or NO, to more complex, like CH_3COOH $(C_2O_2H_4)$.

Weak human bonding can be formed through interactions of members, such as kids from different families in play groups, which may resemble hydrogen bonding in chemical bonding. Likewise, human bonding via various permanent or induced interactions among neighbors, co-workers, and friends may resemble van der Waals' force in chemical bonding. Chemical bonding enables 118 elements to form millions and millions of compounds. Likewise, human bonding enables the formation of countless diverse and distinctive families and communities.

Considering the analogous ways of chemical bonding and human bonding, one may gain some insights for human bonding based on the principles of chemical bonding. For example, if molecules can be formed by charged interaction, ionic bond, then human family can be formed by sexual attraction, which is indeed the case. Interestingly, as in the case of molecules with strong ionic bond but not much covalence, a molecule like Na^+Cl^- will easily dissolve in water. In the same vein, marriage or family formed by sexual attraction may be easily dissolved when environmental conditions change. However, if the couple develops more shared interests and other kind of bonds, like the increased covalence in chemical bonding, then the human bond, like the chemical bond, may be more difficult to separate. Families formed by opposite sexes may resemble chemical bonds with more ionicity, while families formed by gay couples may resemble chemical bond with more covalence. Thus, if stable molecules can be formed by bonds with diverse properties, then analogously one may understand why it is not surprising that stable families can be formed via diverse bonds formed by opposite-sex couples as well as gay couples.

Additionally, weak chemical bonds and weak human bonds may affect group properties analogously. While weak chemical bonds may affect liquefaction, solidification, and water solubility, weak human bonds may affect how a community governs itself, how to respond to emergency or crisis, and so on. The complexity of chemical interactions among molecules can mimic those of human interactions in myriad ways.

Like weak chemical bonding, weaker, non-family human bonding may be classified into several categories: (1) Bonding via economic affinity: people with similar economic status turn to interact with each other. For example, working class families may often interact with each other while doctors and lawyers may interact with each other more easily. (2) Bonding via ethnic and cultural affinity: people of the same ethnic background from the same region may interact with each other more easily and frequently than with those from another region. (3) Bonding via religious or ideological affinity: people of the same religion often interact in churches and temples. Such human bonding, like chemical bonding, can dictate the ways and responses of human populations, in a manner analogous to the ways and responses of chemicals under various conditions.

Just as weak chemical bonding affects the property of compounds, non-family human bonding can affect the characteristics of a human population. For example, non-family human bonding may influence community safety, prosperity, and environment. Non-family human bonding may also determine whether a population wants to be independent, to rebel, or to fight with other populations. The analogies between chemical bonding and human bonding are numerous.

2

THE PARALLEL BETWEEN THE MIXING OF DIFFERENT CHEMICALS AND THE MIXING OF HUMAN POPULATIONS

With the advent of modern science and technology dramatically altering human lives, globalization has become inevitable and unprecedented. How would such dramatic changes alter the trajectory of human history? How can humans modulate these changes to benefit the survival and development of humanity? Perhaps we can gain some useful insights by examining what we have learnt from chemistry and physics and comparing the mixing of human populations with the mixing of chemicals.

Chemical mixtures can be heterogeneous or homogeneous mixtures. Heterogeneous mixtures contain at least two phases that are not uniformly dispersed on a microscopic scale. Homogeneous mixtures contain a single phase in which the components are uniformly distributed. Homogeneous mixtures are solutions. Solutions include gases like air, liquids like gasoline, and solids like gold. The main principle determining how well two or more chemicals form a solution is "like dissolves like." This means molecules with similar molecular polarity, which ranges from completely nonpolar at one end to completely polar (ionic) at the other end. For example, ionic molecules, such as NaCl and $(NH_4)_2SO_4$, dissolve well in water, which is polar.

In liquids and solids, the molecules are held together by a certain amount of intermolecular bonding described in chapter 1, including the hydrogen bond and van der Waals' force. For a solution to occur, the solvent molecules must overcome this intermolecular bonding in the solute and find their way between and around the solute molecules. At the same time, the solvent molecules themselves must be separated from each other by the molecules of the solute. This is achieved best when the bonding forces between the molecules of both components are similar. If bonding forces are sufficiently different, the strongly attracted molecules will cling together, excluding the weakly bonded molecules, and the solute will not dissolve. Oil and water do not mix because the water molecules, strongly attracted to each other, will not allow the weakly attracted oil molecules between them.

Whether two chemicals can mix, as in other chemical and physical reactions, is determined by the laws of thermodynamics. Thermodynamics deals with the relationship between heat, work, temperature, and energy. A thermodynamic system is a precisely defined region of the universe under observation. Everything in the universe except the system is called surroundings. There are open and closed systems. An open system can exchange mass, energy, or both between the system and surroundings. A closed system allows the exchange of energy, but not mass, with its surroundings.

There are several key quantitative measures of a thermodynamic system. The first is enthalpy (H). H is an energy-like property or state function. Its value is determined by temperature, pressure, and the composition of the system, but not by its history. Enthalpy is precisely defined as the sum of the system's internal energy (E) and the product of its pressure (P) and volume (V):

$$H = E + PV.$$

Internal energy is a sum of all microscopic energies including potential and kinetic energies. The second measure is entropy (S). It is defined as a measure of the number of possible microscopic configurations of the individual atoms and molecules of the system (microstates) which correspond to the macroscopic state (macrostate) of the system. Entropy is a measure of disorder of a system. It is a state function of a thermodynamic system. It is a property depending only on the current state of the system, independent of how that state came to be achieved. The second law of thermodynamics states that the entropy of any isolated system always increases.

The third measure is Gibbs free energy (G). It is the energy associated with a chemical or physical reaction that can be used to do work. It combines enthalpy and entropy into a single value:

$$G = H - TS.$$

Because G is a combination of state functions, it is also a state function. G is a thermodynamic potential. It is useful for calculating the maximum reversible work that can be done by a system at constant temperature and pressure. We cannot measure absolute free energy, only free energy change:

$$\Delta G = \Delta H - T\Delta S.$$

ΔG is the difference between the heat released in a reaction and the heat released for the same reaction occurring in a reversible manner. If a system is at equilibrium, $\Delta G = 0$. If the reaction is spontaneous, $\Delta G < 0$. If the reaction is not spontaneous, but is spontaneous in the reverse direction, $\Delta G > 0$. At constant temperature and pressure, ΔG is equal to the maximum amount of work a system can perform on its surroundings while undergoing a spontaneous reaction or change.

During chemical mixing and formation of a solution, molecules or ions of one kind are dispersed throughout a second chemical. This generally increases the disorder and causes an increase in the entropy of the system. When a solution contains the maximum amount of solute that can be dissolved, it is a saturated solution. Otherwise, it is unsaturated. Supersaturated solutions can contain more dissolved solute than the conditions allow and are unstable.

In this case, addition of a seed crystal, a small particle of solute, should cause the excess solute to crystallize. A negative change in H (release of energy) and a positive change in S (increase in freedom or disorder) favor the spontaneous occurrence of a reaction or mixing.

Most solids become more soluble at higher temperatures. As indicated in the equation $\Delta G = \Delta H - T\Delta S$, when T is bigger – $T\Delta S$ will be bigger and make ΔG more negative. This would provide more free energy to drive the mixing reaction or formation of solution. Derivatization, the addition of a functional group to a compound to change its property, is a common technique used in chemistry and pharmacology to improve the solubility of compounds[1].

The concepts and principles of chemical mixing and thermodynamics may provide useful insights for considering the mixing of human populations and behaviors of human populations. The rule, "like dissolves like," may also apply to the mixing of human populations. For example, traditionally, immigrants from the same geographical areas or countries turn to settle in the same places in the USA, forming Chinatown, Koreatown, or little Italy in many cities. Jewish people may live in one area in many cities, while Muslims may live in selected areas in Christian countries, and vice versa.

In the mixing of human populations, the incoming population can be considered analogously as a solute, while the accepting population can be considered as a solvent. As in the case of chemical mixing or dissolution, for mixing to occur the accepting population needs to overcome the non-family affinities in the incoming population and form affinities with members of the incoming population. This may be best done when the bonding affinities among the incoming population are similar to the accepting population. For example, when northern Europeans settle in the USA, they generally mix well with the existing population with European origin, given their shared ethnic, cultural, and religious background.

Like chemicals, if the bonding forces are sufficiently different, the strongly bonded members in the population will stick together, excluding the weakly bonded members of outside population. One striking example may be the Amish population in the USA, who still live in their own isolated areas. Another example is the Hasidic Jewish community in New York City, who live closely together and follow their longtime traditions.

The forces that tie the members of populations together include those three kinds of non-family bonding forces discussed in chapter 1: economic affinity, ethnic/cultural affinity, and religious/ideological affinity. These forces may also change if conditions change and members of populations acquire new characteristics. As functional groups can be added to chemicals to change their solubility, humans may acquire new characters by changing their economic status, their religious/ideological affiliations, and so on.

Human changes akin to derivatization can be observed in various peoples. For example, the early immigrants from China turned to live together in Chinatown and did work relating to restaurants, laundries, and other manual jobs. However, their offspring are often more educated and become more secure economically. They then turn to live in more affluent neighborhoods which may be predominantly white. Similar situations may be observed for African-Americans and Hispanic-Americans. Likewise, changes in religious or ideological affiliations may make people more easily settle in a new society or population. The adoption of communism in Eastern European countries and East Asia also facilitated population mixing in the twentieth century.

To systematically consider these forces and their outcomes in human populations, we may adapt the concepts of thermodynamics to help us understand, analyze, and predict the behaviors of human populations. In a human thermodynamic system, humans may be considered the equivalent of mass in the physical thermodynamic system. Because humans cannot permanently leave Earth, we may consider Earth as a closed system. Additionally, we may consider the concepts of H (enthalpy), entropy (S), free energy (G), and temperature (T) in the human system. The human H (H_h) can be defined as a parameter for the internal community or governing energy in a population, society, or country. The human internal energy (E_h) may be internal community energy from bonding among families, while government forces and pressure may be the equivalent of PV in the physical thermodynamic system. Like chemical H, H_h may be calculated as $E_h + PV_h$.

The human S (S_h) may be defined, similarly to chemicals and compounds, as the degree of disorder or freedom. Humans, like substances, tend to increase the degree of freedom or disorder, in an isolated system. Human G (G_h) may be defined as the net energy needed for a mixing or change to occur. The human T (T_h) can be considered as a general condition indicator of the greater human world, such as the advancement level of science and technology. To consider whether a mixing is favorable, one may also use the following equation:

$$\Delta Gh = \Delta Hh - Th\Delta Sh.$$

If populations in a country or system are at equilibrium, $\Delta G = 0$. If mixing of populations is favorable, $\Delta G < 0$. If the mixing is not favorable, $\Delta G > 0$. If two populations are similar in their non-family bonding, then ΔHh would be close to zero. In this case, the mixing of populations can be driven by the increase in Sh, the degree of freedom or disorder. Consequently, the mixing of two populations would be quite favorable. However, if two populations have different bonding forces, then much energy would be needed to overcome the preexisting bonding forces. In this case, ΔHh would be quite positive, and the mixing would not be favorable. Examples may include those who practice strong religious faith and racial identity are generally disinclined to mix with others but live together in one neighborhood when settling in a new country or population.

The advancement of science and technology has accelerated globalization. Science and technology may be considered as a temperature factor. Advanced technology causes elevated temperature of human conditions, thus increasing the contribution of increased degree of freedom (ΔSh) to make the mixing of populations more favorable. Additionally, community and government energy (Hh) can contribute greatly in making the mixing more or less favorable. For example, the adoption of amnesty would provide a large negative ΔHh to drive population mixing. In contrast, genocidal action, like that committed by the Nazi government in Germany, will provide a large positive ΔHh to drive the mixing to the reverse direction.

The second law of thermodynamics states that the entropy of any isolated system always increases. In other words, without work, the degree of disorder always increases. A parallel phenomenon also occurs with human populations. For example, in China, populations migrated and mixed in many areas throughout the centuries. Consequently, many people of different background mixed in various areas of China, and these populations become quite homogenous in identities and cultures. For example, many Mongolian and Manchurian people settled within the Han populations, changed their names, and adopted the cultures in many regions. Consequently, Chinese people who may have diverse background eventually all considered them the same people and shared the same heritage. Such phenomenon may also be observed in Europe.

On the basis of the thermodynamic theory of human populations, one may gain certain insights and also make some predictions. First, with advanced science and technology—that is, elevated human thermodynamic temperature, Th—changes in the degree of disorder (ΔSh) will have an exaggerated effect. For example, with the use of powerful communication apps like Facebook, Twitter, and WeChat, fake news can be spread very quickly and widely, making unprecedented, dramatic impact on societies and the world. Donald Trump would not have won the 2016 presidential election if it had been held in the last century without the aid of mass communication apps like Twitter. Likewise, these powerful communication tools also aid the mixing of populations. For example, the 2021 quick gathering of Haitian migrants at the Texas border was aided by communication apps. It is worth noting that temperature also increase the rate of reactions. In chemical kinetics or reaction kinetics, the reaction rate constant is calculated using the Arrhenius equation:

$$K = Ae^{-Ea/(RT)}.$$

A is the pre-exponential factor or A-factor, Ea is the activation energy, R is the molar gas constant, and T is the absolute temperature. As indicated by the equation, higher temperature will increase reaction rates. Thus, one may reason that elevated Th will also increase the reaction rates relating to human populations.

Second, with intensified contribution from ΔSh under the advanced technological environment, much more energy, Hh, is needed to maintain equilibrium or to avoid dramatic, undesirable changes in populations and countries. This would mean much more work from societies and governments to counteract the intensified effects of increased degree of human disorder (Sh) to control rapid mixing of populations. Before the industrial revolution, changes in human lives on Earth were slower. After the industrial revolution, changes occurred much more rapidly. The changes caused by internet revolution are dramatic, and the potential for dramatic, adverse effects on humanity as a whole cannot be ignored. The same reasoning also applies to the changes in the physical world on Earth. The terrestrial world had changed slowly for thousands of years before the industrial revolution. It has changed dramatically in the past century or fifty years.

Third, with the intensifying effect of advanced technology, homogenization of human populations may occur more rapidly than one can foresee, since elevated Th will intensify reactions rates. Consequently, the diversity of human populations may disappear, along with the disappearance of diversity of living organisms on Earth. The mixing of human populations would increase the degree of human disorder or freedom (Sh) on Earth, which would be a closed system insofar as human thermodynamics is concerned. Eventually, all human populations on Earth may be homogenized, as happened more or less in China. This may lead to the loss of the diversity of countries, cultures, and heritage.

Fourth, the consideration of thermodynamic theory of human populations may suggest effective ways to influence population mixing. In the early days of the civil rights movement, federal government actions had been very positive in ending segregation. This would be reflected as a strong Hh factor in pushing mixing. Additionally, one may increase the contribution of Hh in mixing by altering bonding affinities in the populations. For example, as African-Americans become more educated and gain higher-paying jobs, they have more bonding affinities with other people with higher-paying jobs and naturally become integrated into neighborhoods where more affluent people reside. This would be a much slower process than quick governmental legal actions. However, such changes would be longlasting and would fundamentally change the status of racial relations.

Changes in a population's bonding affinities may also un-mix a previously mixed population. For example, the former Yugoslavia with multiple ethnic groups existed as one united country under the communism/socialism ideology. However, with the fall of communism, the bonding affinities from shared belief were lost, and Yugoslavia quickly disintegrated into multiple countries based on other, stronger bonding affinities, such as ethnic and religious affinities. A slower but similar process may be occurring in the USA. In the mid-twentieth century, a family with one parent working, whether working class or otherwise, may have been able to support a whole family and live the American dream. However, in recent decades it has been increasingly difficult for working class families to live on one paycheck. Consequently, there is un-mixing among white Americans, European Americans. This is caused by a change in economic affinity. The working-class white families do not share a common economic affinity with the more affluent white families. Consequently, their ways of living and believing have diverged. There is increasing un-mixing among white Americans in their lives and ideologies, which may have accelerated during the Obama presidency. Trump did not create this divide in 2016, but he captured this and manipulated the resentful feelings of these non-liberal whites to gain presidency.

While humans are beginning to recognize the adverse impact of loss of diversity and environmental changes on humanity, the world's push for economic growth and progressive social agenda have the same potential to exert unforeseen, large-scale, adverse effects on the survival and development of humanity as a whole. Under such circumstances, it may be useful to gain some insights about the potential of various human actions to adversely affect human development by analyzing scientifically proven principles of the natural world, including physical entities and living organisms.

The idea of human thermodynamics may apply to many countries/societies to explain and perhaps predict what may happen, because mixing and un-mixing occur most of the time. The equation $\Delta Gh = \Delta Hh - Th\Delta Sh$ indicates that the direction of a society or country is determined by the balance between community and governing energy Hh and the intrinsic property of populations' tendency for freedom/disorder Sh. The founding fathers of the USA were aware of the danger associated with pure democracy and majority rule. Thus, they set up a complex system of governing bodies of representative democracy.

Under elevated human thermodynamic Th, the effects of changes in the degree of disorder or freedom will be exaggerated in influencing the direction of populations, mixing, un-mixing, or related processes. To counteract such exaggerated effects of ΔSh, increased ΔHh may be needed. This may be achieved by increasing government action or community bonding. For example, with the power of mass communications tools like Twitter and Facebook, elections can be influenced easily, and more oversight of these rapid communication tools is necessary to ensure that these tools will not be used to manipulate election results. However, to ensure a positive impact, the oversight needs to be constructed thoughtfully and desirably under the purview of the established legal system, instead of *ad hoc* oversights from CEOs, political groups, and so on.

Further exacerbating the rapid changes and potential impact are the economic and business interests of many countries trying to achieve unlimited economic growth, access unlimited cheap laborers, and obtain cheap consumer products, without any consideration of the long-term effects on Earth and humanity as a whole. Scientifically and logically grounded, strong government actions to guide and modulate the interplay of multiple powerful tools and interests of various communities and countries are necessary to prevent unexpected, drastic adverse effects on societies and countries. However, currently, government actions, even strong, well-intended government actions, are often guided by short-term interests or emotionally charged hyperboles, not by proven principles or thoughtful long-term strategies. For example, the promotion of renewal energy often does not match up with the reality. How do you make wind power when there is no wind? How do you promote clean energy by using electricity when so much electricity is still generated from coal? How does one promote social justice and equality when some countries take talented people from struggling countries and leave the majority of the people in these countries to suffer in vain? Can a country like the USA save all struggling people in the world by taking away talented people in other countries?

In mathematical terms, the quickly increasing Th is making the contribution of ThΔSh much bigger now than two hundred or even fifty years ago in influencing ΔGh or the direction of countries and the world at large. Thus, ΔHh, or community and government energy, needs to intensify promptly to counteract potential adverse effects on ΔGh. Clearly, strong, unifying government actions are necessary for the continued existence and wellbeing of humanity on Earth, but there is a lack of guiding principles. A unifying theory to explain and model the behavior and trajectory of human populations is vital for the long-term survival and development of humanity, in this new era of advanced science and technology.

1. Wang SY, Shi XC, Laborda P. 2020. Indole-based melatonin analogues: Synthetic approaches and biological activity. *Eur J Med Chem* 185: 111847

3

VIEWS FROM BIOLOGY: THE IMPORTANCE OF GENETIC DIVERSITY AND VARIATION

Biological diversity is the variety and variability of living organisms on Earth. Biodiversity includes variations at three levels: genetic, species, and ecosystem. Although more than 99.9 percent of all species that lived on Earth are estimated to be extinct, more than ten million species are currently estimated to be alive. The global community has become more and more aware of the importance of maintaining biodiversity in the survival and development of humanity. Many studies and documents have been published regarding biodiversity. Here, I would like to consider genetic diversity and variation, which provides a molecular basis for biological diversity.

Biological sciences differ from physical sciences in that biology deals with living beings. Biological sciences aim to understand life at the organismic, molecular, and cellular levels. Living organisms can be unicellular or multicellular organisms; all living organisms consist of one or more cells. These cells consist of four types of macromolecular building blocks: nucleic acids, including DNA (deoxyribonucleic acid) and RNA (ribonucleic acid); proteins; lipids; and glycans[1]. DNA and RNA are produced from 8 nucleosides. Proteins are synthesized from 20 natural amino acids. There are eight categories of lipids, and glycans are derived from at least thirty-two saccharides. DNA is the hereditary or genetic material of cells. DNA are composed of four bases: A, T, C, and G. The DNA in all cells contains stretches which encode for specific proteins or RNA. Each amino acid in proteins is encoded by a codon containing three bases.

Genome size is the amount of DNA contained in a haploid genome. Genome sizes of bacteriophages and viruses vary from about two kilobases to over one million bases. The genomes of prokaryotes range from ~five hundred kilobases to ~twelve million bases. Prokaryotes are unicellular organisms that lack nuclear membrane-enclosed nucleus. The genomes of eukaryotes range from ~ten million bases in fungi to >one hundred billion bases in certain plants, salamanders, and lungfishes. Eukaryotes are organisms whose cells have a nucleus enclosed within a nuclear envelope. Humans and animals are all eukaryotes. Human genome contains twenty-three chromosomes and 3.1 billion bases.

To make proteins and enzymes, cells first transcribe DNA into messenger RNA (mRNA). Then, proteins are made from mRNA by ribosomes. Enzymes are proteins that catalyze specific chemical reactions in and outside of cells. Proteins and enzymes carry out the synthesis of all biological molecules in cells. Enzymatic reactions differ from regular chemical reactions in several aspects: Enzymatic reactions can occur much faster due to the catalytic activity provided by enzymes; enzymatic reactions are generally much more specific, with far less byproducts due to the specific substrate binding sites in enzymes; and many thermodynamically unfavorable enzymatic reactions, such as biosynthesis of molecules, are driven by coupling with the hydrolysis of cellular energy, ATP.

The proliferation of organisms and cells requires DNA replication, which is error-prone. The rate at which DNA polymerase adds incorrect nucleotides during DNA replication is a major factor in determining the spontaneous mutation rate in living organisms. Spontaneous mutation rates vary greatly among organisms[2]. Mutation rates in microbes are about 1/300 per genome per replication, while mutation rates in higher eukaryotes are estimated to be 0.1–100 per genome per sexual generation. A whole genome study estimated the human intergeneration mutation rate of about 1.1 x 10^{-8} per position per haploid genome[3].

In lower organisms such as unicellular organisms, one can easily observe the effects of spontaneous mutations. A good example is the well-studied yeast *Saccharomyces cerevisiae*, which is used in winemaking, baking, and brewing. One can make laboratory strains that do not grow in medium without a nutrient, for example an amino acid. However, one can grow these cells in medium without the nutrient and look for natural revertants that can grow without the nutrient. In general, more than one revertants may be found for every one million cells plated on solid medium. This is because these cells can spontaneously acquire genetic mutations that allow the cells to grow in the absence of the nutrient.

In 1998, Rutherford and Linquist[4] showed that artificially reducing levels of heat shock protein 90 (Hsp90) chaperone induces a wide variety of phenotypes. Deficient levels of Hsp90 in fruit fly *Drosophila* reveals diverse developmental phenotypes in abdomen, bristles, eyes, halters, legs, thorax, and wings, such as black facets in one eye, notched wings, and deformed legs. When they repeated the experiment in different strains of flies, each of which has a different genetic background, it led to different Hsp90-dependent phenotypes. They suggested that Hsp90 is an evolutionary "capacitor" that creates robustness to buffer the effects of mutations, allowing genetic variation to accumulate in a cryptic form, to be released when Hsp90 capacity is compromised later.

Subsequently, studies in diverse organisms have shown that Hsp90 broadly influences the phenotypic manifestation of genetic diversity. In the plant *Arabidopsis thaliana*, inhibition of Hsp90 by geldanamycin reveals phenotypes including disruption of typical symmetry and oval-shaped, flat leaves[5]. The authors suggested that Hsp90 has an important role in many aspects of developmental plasticity, that these roles vary in different genetic backgrounds, and that the dependencies of different pathways on Hsp90 segregate independently of each other. In zebrafish, partial inhibition of Hsp90 was shown to be associated with specific developmental abnormalities[6]. Administration of specific drugs at defined times in early development for the limited reduction of Hsp90 activity showed that different cryptic genetic variants could be revealed consistently in genetically distinct fish strains. The study suggested that mild perturbation of Hsp90 function at critical developmental stages causes the variable penetrance and expressivity of many developmental anomalies.

In the yeast Saccharomyces cerevisiae, Jarosz and Lindquist[7] showed that Hsp90 operates on roughly 20 percent of the preexisting genetic variation to both preserve phenotypic robustness and provide a broad conduit to diversification. Environmental stress creates a dynamic interface for transitioning between these effects. Half of the traits buffered by Hsp90 and half potentiated by it had beneficial effects on growth; the other half were detrimental. In the cavefish *Astyanax mexicanus*, it was shown that Hsp90 masks standing-eye size variation in surface populations of the fish[8]. A study of more than 1,500 disease-causing mutants in humans[9] showed that Hsp90 buffers mutant phenotype and rescues the function of the Fanconi Anemia pathway by binding and stabilizing mutated proteins.

Genetic variation or tumor heterogeneity is widely observed in various cancers. There are several levels of heterogeneity or variation in cancers[10]. First, genetic and functional heterogeneity exist among tumors of different patients. For example, some breast cancer patients have mutations in the *BRCA1* gene, while many others do not. Likewise, some lung cancer patients have mutations in the *EGFR* gene, while others may have mutations in the *LKB1* gene. Second, there is heterogeneity among cells of one tumor, that is, intratumor heterogeneity[11]. Intratumor heterogeneity is a major factor determining the development of drug resistance and therapeutic outcomes in cancer patients. Third, there is heterogeneity among different metastatic lesions of the same patient. Even when tumors in distant sites originated from a common ancestor, different tumor microenvironment can induce variations in different distant sites after the initial colonization. Finally, there is also heterogeneity among the cells of an individual metastasis. These variations and heterogeneity enable tumor cells to become very adaptive to the environment and acquire resistance to therapeutic treatments.

Genetic variation and diversity provide a survival advantage for species, because the variations enable the species to adapt to changes in the environment while maintaining the survival of the population. The heterogeneity in tumors, genetic and functional, enables tumors to progress aggressively and become drug resistant, which presents a revealing case for the survival advantage that variations can provide. In humans, genetic variations that may cause diseases under one circumstance may provide survival advantage under another circumstance. Below, I explain two such cases.

The first case is sickle-cell anemia, which is caused by a mutation in the gene that encodes hemoglobin (Hb), the oxygen-carrying molecule in our blood. Adult hemoglobin is made of two α and two β globin chains. Sickle hemoglobin (HbS) contains a Glu to Val mutation at residue #6 of the β globin chain[12]. Every person has two copies of the gene encoding the globin chain. Hemozygotes for sickle hemoglobin with two affected β globin chains develop sickle cell disease. Hemoglobin with two HbS chains polymerize and cause red blood cells to sickle and occlude blood vessels. Heterozygotes for sickle hemoglobin have sickle cell trait and are generally asymptomatic[13].

It was puzzling why sickle cell anemia was so prevalent in some African populations. In some regions, nearly 40 percent of the population carries at least one HbS gene. How could such a bad mutation that sometimes causes lethal sickle cell anemia persist in such a high frequency if it does not offer some survival advantage? In the 1940s, doctors began to recognize that sickle cell anemia provides protection against malaria. Numerous studies have shown that HbS carriers have strong protection against malaria[14]. A meta-analysis examining forty-four studies of children with HbS showed significant protection from severe malaria syndromes, including greater than 90 percent protection from severe malaria, cerebral malaria and severe malarial anemia[15]. Multiple molecular mechanisms have been suggested to explain the protection against malaria conferred by HbS carriers. One important mechanism may be enhanced immune response in HbS carriers in response to malaria[14].

The second case is hereditary hemochromatosis, which is most commonly the consequence of mutations in the HFE gene[16]. The mutations cause the absorption of more iron than is required, which can result in the impairment of organ structure and function. The HFE mutation Cys282Tyr is pathologically most relevant and occurs in the Caucasian population with a carrier frequency of up to one in eight in specific European regions. Currently, approximately 0.4 percent of Caucasians carry a homozygous and approximately

6 percent a heterozygous *HFE* Cys282Tyr mutation[17, 18]. Large-scale population studies have revealed that most HFE mutation carriers with a mild iron-overload phenotype lack any clinically relevant disease symptoms.

The fact that the Cys282Tyr mutation is frequent but causes a disease-related phenotype only in a subset of carriers suggests that this HFE variant may offer certain survival advantages. For example, increased iron uptake may have helped humans to better cope with a grain-based diet lacking red meat. Recent studies have suggested that the HFE variant can positively influence the immune system, general fitness, and reproductive abilities of the carriers. It was shown that 80 percent of successful French athletes carry a heterozygous HFE mutation[19]. It was suggested that enhanced iron supply in the carriers leads to the superior physical performance of these athletes. Two large-scale studies among the Sicilian population showed that HFE C282Y heterozygous individuals, particularly women, carrying one copy of the Cys282Tyr variant, have a significantly increased life expectancy compared to controls[20,21].

Furthermore, recent studies in humans have shown that genetic diversity, specifically genomic heterozygosity (the condition of having two different alleles at a genetic locus), is a predictor of mortality and provides survival advantage[22, 23]. Likewise, heterozygote advantage has been observed in diverse organisms ranging from plants to mammals[24–28]. Overwhelming evidence shows that genetic variation and diversity is advantageous for the survival of virtually all living organisms at the levels of both individuals and species.

The biological insurance theory crystallizes the

importance of biodiversity. The biological insurance theory is supported by ample experimental tests and field studies[29]. The theory identifies two ways by which biodiversity can enhance ecosystem functioning: buffering effect and performance-enhancing effect. In buffering effect, biodiversity would reduce variability of aggregate ecosystem properties that arise from species' differential responses to environmental variations. In performance-enhancing effect, biodiversity would increase the mean level of ecosystem properties as the best-performing species are favored under each environmental condition.

With the tools of synthetic biology, scientists are capable of creating viruses and independent organisms that acquire unknown functions. In 2005, a team of CDC researchers and their colleagues successfully reconstructed the Spanish flu virus that caused the 1918–19 flu pandemic, which caused the deaths of up to fifty million people worldwide[30]. In 2016, genomics entrepreneur Craig Venter and his colleagues created a synthetic cell that contains the smallest genome of any known, independent organism[31]. This genome, JCVI-syn3.0, contains 531 kilobase pairs and encodes 438 proteins and 35 annotated RNAs. JCVI-syn3.0 has a doubling time of about 180 minutes. In 2019, Jason Chin and his colleagues at the Medical Research Council of Molecular Biology in Britain created a living organism whose DNA is entirely human-made[32]. They created a variant of *Escherichia coli* with a four million base pair synthetic genome. The team recoded 18,214 codons to create an organism with a 61-codon genome, not the natural 64-codon genome. There are twenty amino acids naturally, and each amino acid is coded by a three-base code in DNA.

The genomes of betacoronaviruses and SAR-CoV-2 are large and range from twenty-seven to thirty-two kilobases in size. Nonetheless, with the power of synthetic biology, scientists are fully capable of designing and creating such viruses with ease. Furthermore, with the power of genome editing tool CRISPR (clustered regularly interspaced short palindromic repeats), scientists can edit and modify the genomes of many cells and organisms[33]. However, the potential for unwanted genetic changes is also great[34].

Synthetic biology and genome editing can add to the biodiversity on Earth. However, the creation of novel organisms and viruses can cause catastrophic events, particularly in light of the COVID-19 pandemic. While leaking of infectious agents from research and clinical labs is generally rare, it can happen anywhere in the world and has happened. For example, in a 2009 article, Singh documented an array of laboratory-acquired infections, including bacteria, virus, fungi, and parasites[35]. Between the years 1976–1978, there were over one thousand cases of laboratory-associated infections and more than forty deaths worldwide.

Pedrosa and Cardoso reviewed 141 articles relating to accidental viral infections by hospital or laboratory workers[36]. They analyzed sixty-six articles, with thirty-one reporting hospital infections accounting for 241 infections. Thirty-five articles are related to 219 laboratory infections. They found that 84 percent of the arboviral infections in laboratories were airborne, while 16 percent were acquired percutaneously. Aerosol inhalation was also the mode of infection for

77 percent of laboratory infections by blood-borne viruses[36]. In summary, it is well documented that laboratory-acquired infections relating to pathogenic agents—particularly emerging viruses such as SARS, Marbug, West Nile virus, and Zika—is a serious risk and should be prevented through the implementation of nationally and internationally certified protocols[37, 38].

It is not a matter of whether any synthetic materials can be leaked, but when. There will always be human errors. There are also many unknown unknowns, particularly when it concerns living organisms. Life is extremely plastic and can always find a way, as discussed above. Synthetic materials, once released, can be combined genetically with naturally occurring living organisms in the wild, and the results can be very unpredictable. The loss of natural biodiversity coupled with the potential danger of synthetic viruses and organisms can pose grave threats to the survival of humanity.

It is also worth mentioning that the loss of biodiversity is currently accompanied by the loss of diversity and variation in many other aspects of human life on Earth. The effects of such loss of diversity have not been considered. Here I would like to point out some of these losses. First, there is a loss of diverse viewpoints in countries all over the world. The predominant views in many influential countries including the USA and Western countries are the extreme right and the extreme left. People are pushed to the right or the left to adopt extreme views with little diversity or variation. Second, there is a loss of diversity and variation in governance. To gain control and dominance in the world, the Western powers have consistently pushed for countries to adopt liberal democracy regardless of the cultural and political background in specific countries and societies. As a result, many countries, including those in Africa, Middle East, and Latin America, have become chaotic without fully functional, effective governments for the people.

Third, with globalization and the tendency to push for open borders, there is a loss of diversity and variation in the cultural and ethnic makeups of countries. With the progressives' push for globalization and mass immigration, more and more countries may be on track to become a cosmopolitan, generic country with similar foods, culture, and ethnic makeups. This would diminish the diversity and variations of countries.

These losses of diversity are further compounded by the fact that despite the lack of diversity in many aspects, the people in the world do not have a common, shared moral and ethical compass. While Earth is extremely diverse physically and biologically, the physical and biological world is governed by the same scientific principles of mathematics, physics, chemistry, molecular biology, and genetics. Regardless of religious beliefs, all people must follow the fundamental principles of mathematics, physics, and chemistry to build buildings and bridges, generate electricity, or make cars and other machineries. Regardless of social views or beliefs, people need antibiotics for treatment of bacterial infections, and an egg and a sperm must come together to form a zygote, *in vivo* or *in vitro*, to make a baby. Under the unifying principles of mathematics, physics, chemistry, and biology, the world became extremely diverse without human interference.

Likewise, to maintain and develop diversity and variation to sustain humanity, it is necessary to have shared guiding principles, namely a fundamental moral and ethical code. With rapidly advancing technologies and changing environment on Earth, a common moral code encouraging the pursuit of equity and justice will be critical for the survival of humanity and for sustaining and developing diversity in all aspects of human life: culture, governance, technology, and environment. The pursuit of freedom should be under the framework of equality and justice. Without a common, unifying moral and ethical code, different groups of human populations will always try to eliminate each other's ideology and existence and dominate, as shown in over three thousand years of human history and exemplified by crusades and genocides occurred between different religious/racial groups throughout history.

Like the natural world, the social world can operate under a set of unifying moral and ethical principles while achieving maximum diversity and variation. As discussed in chapter 2, the increasing human Sh drives the humanity system to mix and achieve homogeneity as in the case of formation of a solution. Especially in the era of advanced science and technology (high Th), the contribution of ΔSh is exaggerated. To maintain diversity and variation, much more community and government energy (ΔHh) guided by a moral code is necessary. With a unifying moral code, the human world can flourish with diverse cultures, arts, ideologies, and environments. All cultures and ideologies should be able to thrive, just as all kinds of buildings and architectures can be built using the same laws of mathematics and physics.

Humans have become aware of diminishing biological diversity and the importance of maintaining that diversity. However, there is little awareness or consideration of the adverse effects of globalization and loss of diversity in the social world on the survival and development of humanity as a whole. With the advancement of science and technology, the impact of both negative and positive events, such as the spread of infectious agents like COVID-19, is accelerated and exaggerated. To minimize the occurrence of irreversible adverse events that can cause catastrophic results for the existence of humanity, there is a need to deliberately control and slow down certain aspects of globalization and social changes. Note that globalization includes the movement of goods and that of people. The movement of goods are much more easily controlled, started, accelerated, decreased, reversed, or stopped with relative ease. However, any changes in the human population movement can be much more difficult and painful. For example, un-mixing of human populations may involve genocides. Thus, much more energy should be applied to regulate the movement of humans, but not necessarily goods.

Does the human population have to forever increase in order to keep the economy growing? Should humanity continue to enable and encourage the uncontrolled competition among countries such that resources on Earth are being depleted rapidly? Should humanity deliberately slow down industrial progress and try to maintain the lifestyle already achieved for some time to come? Changes were slow on Earth before the industrial revolution. However, with the rapid advancement of technologies such as biotech and computation, humanity is on a runaway bullet train that may be running towards a cliff. Would it be beneficial to arrest the current advance of technologies and for humanity to pause in history for a couple of thousand years, like the period prior to the industrial revolution? We may continue to consider these questions in later chapters.

1.　Marth JD. 2008. A unified vision of the building blocks of life. *Nat Cell Biol* 10: 1015–6

2.　Drake JW, Charlesworth B, Charlesworth D, Crow JF. 1998. Rates of spontaneous mutation. *Genetics* 148: 1667–86

3.　Roach JC, Glusman G, Smit AF, Huff CD, Hubley R, Shannon PT, Rowen L, Pant KP, Goodman N, Bamshad M, Shendure J, Drmanac R, Jorde LB, Hood L, Galas DJ. 2010. Analysis of genetic inheritance in a family quartet by whole-genome sequencing. *Science* 328: 636–9

4.　Rutherford SL, Lindquist S. 1998. Hsp90 as a capacitor for morphological evolution. *Nature* 396: 336–42

5.　Queitsch C, Sangster TA, Lindquist S. 2002. Hsp90 as a capacitor of phenotypic variation. *Nature* 417: 618–24

6.　Yeyati PL, Bancewicz RM, Maule J, van Heyningen V. 2007. Hsp90 Selectively Modulates Phenotype in Vertebrate Development. *PLOS Genetics* 3: e43

7.　Jarosz DF, Lindquist S. 2010. Hsp90 and environmental stress transform the adaptive value of natural genetic variation. *Science* 330: 1820–4

8.　Rohner N, Jarosz DF, Kowalko JE, Yoshizawa M, Jeffery WR, Borowsky RL, Lindquist S, Tabin CJ. 2013. Cryptic variation in morphological evolution: HSP90 as a capacitor for loss of eyes in cavefish. *Science* 342: 1372–5

9.　Karras GI, Yi S, Sahni N, Fischer M, Xie J, Vidal M, D'Andrea AD, Whitesell L, Lindquist S. 2017. HSP90 Shapes the Consequences of Human Genetic Variation. *Cell* 168: 856–66 e12

10. Baliu-Piqué M, Pandiella A, Ocana A. 2020. Breast Cancer Heterogeneity and Response to Novel Therapeutics. *Cancers* 12: 3271

11. Black JRM, McGranahan N. 2021. Genetic and non-genetic clonal diversity in cancer evolution. *Nat Rev Cancer* 21: 379–92

12. Ingram VM. 1959. Abnormal human haemoglobins. III. The chemical difference between normal and sickle cell haemoglobins. *Biochim Biophys Acta* 36: 402–11

13. Bunn HF. 1997. Pathogenesis and treatment of sickle cell disease. *N Engl J Med* 337: 762–9

14. Gong L, Parikh S, Rosenthal PJ, Greenhouse B. 2013. Biochemical and immunological mechanisms by which sickle cell trait protects against malaria. *Malar J* 12: 317

15. Taylor SM, Parobek CM, Fairhurst RM. 2012. Haemoglobinopathies and the clinical epidemiology of malaria: a systematic review and meta-analysis. *Lancet Infect Dis* 12: 457–68

16. Hollerer I, Bachmann A, Muckenthaler MU. 2017. Pathophysiological consequences and benefits of HFE mutations: 20 years of research. *Haematologica* 102: 809–17

17. Adams PC, Reboussin DM, Barton JC, McLaren CE, Eckfeldt JH, McLaren GD, Dawkins FW, Acton RT, Harris EL, Gordeuk VR, Leiendecker-Foster C, Speechley M, Snively BM, Holup JL, Thomson E, Sholinsky P, Hemochromatosis, Iron Overload Screening Study Research I. 2005. Hemochromatosis and iron-overload screening in a racially diverse population. *N Engl J Med* 352: 1769–78

18. European Association for the Study of the Liver. 2010. EASL clinical practice guidelines for HFE hemochromatosis. *J Hepatol* 53: 3–22

19. Hermine O, Dine G, Genty V, Marquet LA, Fumagalli G, Tafflet M, Guillem F, Van Lierde F, Rousseaux-Blanchi MP, Palierne C, Lapostolle JC, Cervetti JP, Frey A, Jouven X, Noirez P, Toussaint JF. 2015. Eighty percent of French sport winners in Olympic, world and European competitions have mutations in the hemochromatosis HFE gene. *Biochimie* 119: 1–5

20. Balistreri CR, Candore G, Almasio P, Di Marco V, Colonna-Romano G, Craxi A, Motta M, Piazza G, Malaguarnera M, Lio D, Caruso C. 2002. Analysis of hemochromatosis gene mutations in the Sicilian population: implications for survival and longevity. *Arch Gerontol Geriatr Suppl* 8: 35–42

21. Lio D, Balistreri CR, Colonna-Romano G, Motta M, Franceschi C, Malaguarnera M, Candore G, Caruso C. 2002. Association between the MHC class I gene HFE polymorphisms and longevity: a study in Sicilian population. *Genes Immun* 3: 20–4

22. Bihlmeyer NA, Brody JA, Smith AV, Lunetta KL, Nalls M, Smith JA, Tanaka T, Davies G, Yu L, Mirza SS, Teumer A, Coresh J, Pankow JS, Franceschini N, Scaria A, Oshima J, Psaty BM, Gudnason V, Eiriksdottir G, Harris TB, Li H, Karasik D, Kiel DP, Garcia M, Liu Y, Faul JD, Kardia SL, Zhao W, Ferrucci L, Allerhand M, Liewald DC, Redmond P, Starr JM, De Jager PL, Evans DA, Direk N, Ikram MA, Uitterlinden A, Homuth G, Lorbeer R, Grabe HJ, Launer L, Murabito JM, Singleton AB, Weir DR, Bandinelli S, Deary IJ, Bennett DA, Tiemeier H, Kocher T, Lumley T, Arking DE. 2014. Genetic diversity is a predictor of mortality in humans. *BMC Genet* 15: 159

23. Xu K, Kosoy R, Shameer K, Kumar S, Liu L, Readhead B, Belbin GM, Lee HC, Chen R, Dudley JT. 2019. Genome-wide analysis indicates association between heterozygote advantage and healthy aging in humans. *BMC Genet* 20: 52

24. O'Brien SJ, Roelke ME, Marker L, Newman A, Winkler CA, Meltzer D, Colly L, Evermann JF, Bush M, Wildt DE. 1985. Genetic basis for species vulnerability in the cheetah. *Science* 227: 1428–34

25. Sommer S. 2005. The importance of immune gene variability (MHC) in evolutionary ecology and conservation. *Front Zool* 2: 16

26. Kovach MJ, McCouch SR. 2008. Leveraging natural diversity: back through the bottleneck. *Curr Opin Plant Biol* 11: 193–200

27. Garcia AA, Wang S, Melchinger AE, Zeng ZB. 2008. Quantitative trait loci mapping and the genetic basis of heterosis in maize and rice. *Genetics* 180: 1707–24

28. Foerster K, Delhey K, Johnsen A, Lifjeld JT, Kempenaers B. 2003. Females increase offspring heterozygosity and fitness through extra-pair matings. *Nature* 425: 714–7

29. Loreau M, Barbier M, Filotas E, Gravel D, Isbell F, Miller SJ, Montoya JM, Wang S, Aussenac R, Germain R, Thompson PL, Gonzalez A, Dee LE. 2021. Biodiversity as insurance: from concept to measurement and application. *Biol Rev Camb Philos Soc* 96: 2333–54

30. Tumpey TM, Basler CF, Aguilar PV, Zeng H, Solorzano A, Swayne DE, Cox NJ, Katz JM, Taubenberger JK, Palese P, Garcia-Sastre A. 2005. Characterization of the reconstructed 1918 Spanish influenza pandemic virus. *Science* 310: 77–80

31. Hutchison CA, 3rd, Chuang RY, Noskov VN, Assad-Garcia N, Deerinck TJ, Ellisman MH, Gill J, Kannan K, Karas BJ, Ma L, Pelletier JF, Qi ZQ, Richter RA, Strychalski EA, Sun L, Suzuki Y, Tsvetanova B, Wise KS, Smith HO, Glass JI, Merryman C, Gibson DG, Venter JC. 2016. Design and synthesis of a minimal bacterial genome. *Science* 351: aad6253

32. Fredens J, Wang K, de la Torre D, Funke LFH, Robertson WE, Christova Y, Chia T, Schmied WH, Dunkelmann DL, Beranek V, Uttamapinant C, Llamazares AG, Elliott TS, Chin JW. 2019. Total synthesis of Escherichia coli with a recoded genome. *Nature* 569: 514–8

33. Khatibi S, Sahebkar A, Aghaee-Bakhtiari SH. 2021. CRISPR Genome Editing Technology and its Application in Genetic Diseases: A Review. *Curr Pharm Biotechnol* 22: 468–79

34. Ledford H. 2020. CRISPR gene editing in human embryos wreaks chromosomal mayhem. *Nature* 583: 17–8

35. Singh K. 2009. Laboratory-acquired infections. *Clin Infect Dis* 49: 142–7

36. Pedrosa PB, Cardoso TA. 2011. Viral infections in workers in hospital and research laboratory settings: a comparative review

of infection modes and respective biosafety aspects. *Int J Infect Dis* 15: e366–76

37. Artika IM, Ma'roef CN. 2017. Laboratory biosafety for handling emerging viruses. *Asian Pac J Trop Biomed* 7: 483–91

38. Peng H, Bilal M, Iqbal HMN. 2018. Improved Biosafety and Biosecurity Measures and/or Strategies to Tackle Laboratory-Acquired Infections and Related Risks. *Int J Environ Res Public Health* 15

4

INSIGHTS FROM PROBABILITY THEORY AND STATISTICS: THE IMPORTANCE OF NORMAL DISTRIBUTION IN UNDERSTANDING HUMAN POPULATIONS

Many events in the world seem to happen randomly and with great uncertainty. For example, when does one get into a traffic accident or witness a crime? What number does one get when throwing a pair of dice? Where will lightning strike during a storm? However, the study of probability theory has shown us that there is certainty among uncertainty and that there is a deterministic tendency in stochastic events.

The most important statistical distribution is arguably the normal distribution. The normal distribution was first associated with the analysis of errors of measurements made in astronomical observations. Galileo Galilei (1564–1642) noted that the measurement errors tended to be symmetric and that small errors occurred more frequently than large errors. The normal distribution curve was also discovered by Abraham de Moivre (1667-1754). de Moivre was consulting for gamblers and worked on the probability of coin flips. He noted that as the number of coin flips increased, the shape of the binomial distribution approached a very smooth curve, which is the normal curve. The figure below shows the binomial distribution for twelve coin flips. The smooth curve is the normal distribution. The heights of the vertical lines show binomial probabilities. The normal curve closely approximates the binomial probabilities.

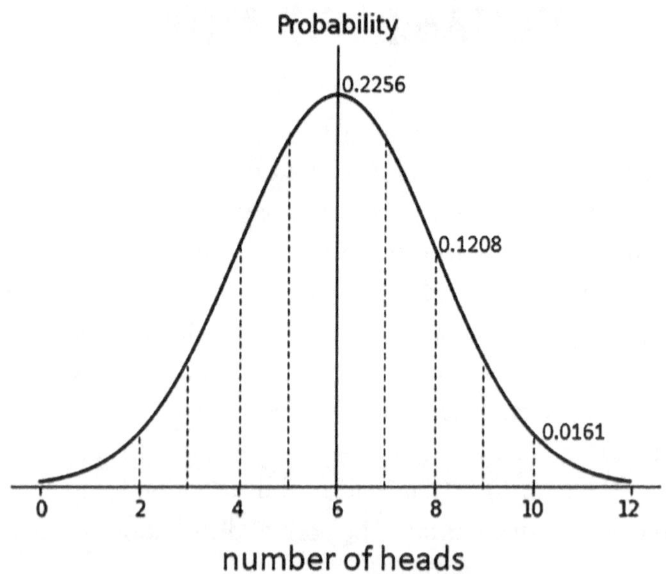

In the beginning of the nineteenth century, Adrien-Marie Legendre (1752–1833) and Carl Friedrich Gauss (1777–1855) worked out the precise mathematical formula for the normal distribution. Gauss also showed that the normal curve provides a close fit to the empirical distribution of observational errors. The same distribution was also discovered by Pierre-Simon Laplace (1749–1827) when he worked on the central limit theorem. The central limit theorem explains why the normal distribution arises so commonly and why the normal distribution approximates generally the mean of a collection of data. The central limit theorem states that the sample mean distribution of a random variable will assume a near-normal or normal distribution if the sample size is large enough.

The normal distribution is a symmetrical, continuous distribution. It is symmetric from the peak of the curve, where the mean is. The normal distribution has two important parameters: the mean, μ, describing the position, and the standard deviation, σ, describing the spread (see the figure below). A normal distribution always has a characteristic bell curve. It is also called the Gaussian distribution. In a perfect normal distribution, $\mu \pm \sigma$ contains 68.26% of the observations; $\mu \pm 2\sigma$ contains 95.46% of the observations; and $\mu \pm 3\sigma$ contains 99.74% of the observations. *Skewness* and *kurtosis* are two types of departure from normality. Skewness means that one tail of the bell curve is drawn out more than the other. Kurtosis is a measure of the flatness of a distribution.

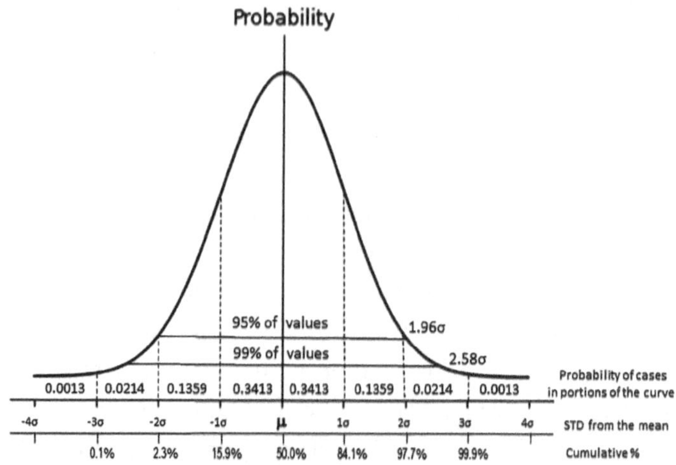

It is unlikely that a data set is perfectly normally distributed. Various statistical tests, such as the Kolmogorov-Smirnov test, can be used to determine whether a data set differs significantly from a normal distribution. If a data set is significantly different from normal, then a transformation, such as logarithmic or square root, can be applied, so that the distribution may become normal. In modern life sciences, the normal distribution is widely used as the statistical basis for determining statistical significance in measurements of many biological activities, such as protein levels and the efficacy of drugs in suppressing cancer cells and tumors[1,2].

Adolphe Quetelet (1796–1874) applied the normal distribution to characteristics of human populations or social science[3,4]. His goal was to understand the statistical laws underlying social phenomena such as crime rates, marriage rates, or suicide rates. Quetelet pioneered a new, mathematical way of understanding the relationship between human height and weight, the height-weight measure, which we know as the body mass index today[5]. Using data from soldiers, Quetelet showed that many physical measurements, such as height, are distributed according to the normal curve. These normally distributed traits are called quantitative traits, including weight, height, and blood pressure.

In 1918, Ronald A Fisher (1890–1962) hypothesized that if several genes affect a trait, the trait will be normally distributed as a quantitative trait[6], which provided the founding principle of quantitative genetics. Many human abilities are quantitative traits. For example, human intelligence is a quantitative trait[7]. Intelligence is a normally distributed trait with a positive end of high performance and a negative end of intellectual disability. The intelligence quotient (IQ) score is often used to measure intelligence. The average score on an IQ test is 100. One standard deviation in modern IQ testing is 15 points. An IQ score between 85 and 115 is considered average. An IQ score of 130 or above is considered a superior level, and an IQ score below 70 would be considered intellectually disabled. Likewise, SAT and ACT scores are normally distributed quantitative traits. In 2017, in the US the SAT score mean was 1060 with a standard deviation of 195. During 2020–2021 reporting year, the ACT score mean was 20.7 with a standard deviation of 5.9 in the US.

Most human traits are under the influence of multiple genetic and environmental factors and are thus quantitative traits. Interestingly, a study of resilience to cancer showed that it is aquantitative trait[8]. Toledano–Toledano and colleagues carried out a study of 330 family caregivers of children with cancer hospitalized at the National Institute of Health in Mexico City[8]. The resilience of caregivers was measured by using the Mexican Scale of Resilience (RESIM) score. The RESIM total score was shown to be normally distributed. Another interesting study involves the measurement of social capital[9]. Primack and colleagues developed a brief measure of social capital among early career clinical researchers. The study of 414 clinical research trainees at the University of Pittsburgh in 2007–2012 showed that social capital is normally distributed with a mean of 6.4 (10–point scale) and a standard deviation of 1.7. Social capital was found to be significantly associated with sex, age, confidence in research skills, work-related motivation, burnout, and social support. Another study investigated the quantitative traits of mice[10]. Zhou and colleagues measured the anatomic, blood chemical, and blood hematological parameters (a total of twenty-seven phenotypes) in 170 eight-to-ten-week-old wild-type mice. These phenotypes were shown to be normally distributed.

The twenty-first century has brought about many powerful genomics technologies, including genome-wide association studies (GWAS). A GWAS is an approach that rapidly scans markers across the complete set of genomes of many people to find genetic variations associated with a particular disease[11–15]. These GWAS studies have shown that common disorders such as obesity, hypertension, and dementia are associated with multiple genes of small effect size[16]. Common disorders are the extremes of relevant quantitative traits or the quantitative extremes of continuous distributions of genetic risk. For example, a deep post-GWAS analysis of risk variants associated with Alzheimer's disease (AD) identified over 300 AD risk genes and over 200 risk regions[17]. GWAS studies have also identified multiple risk genes for cardiovascular diseases such as hypertension, coronary artery disease, atrial fibrillation, and dyslipidemia[18]. A meta-analysis of GWAS data sets of European ancestry with 62892 type 2 diabetes (T2D) cases and 596,424 controls along with gene expression data identified thirty-three functional risk genes[19]. Three of the genes are targeted by approved drugs. These results all support the idea that common disorders are extremes of quantitative traits.

Clearly, modern science and technology have validated and extended many concepts proposed many years ago. It is amazing that the distribution of errors of measurement in astronomical observations follows the same curve as human traits and presumably many traits of other living organisms. This is in complete agreement with the idea that human bonding and chemical bonding follow analogous principles. At the higher abstract level, many principles that govern the universe, physical or living, may be parallel or analogous.

Education and training will improve many human traits or skills, including intellectual skills like test taking and physical skills like running. Thus, education and training are important for elevating the economic and social status of disadvantaged communities such as minorities and those in rural areas. For a population, education and training would move the whole distribution curve of quantitative traits, such as ACT and SAT scores, to higher values. The shape of distribution would likely not change much, as illustrated in the figure below.

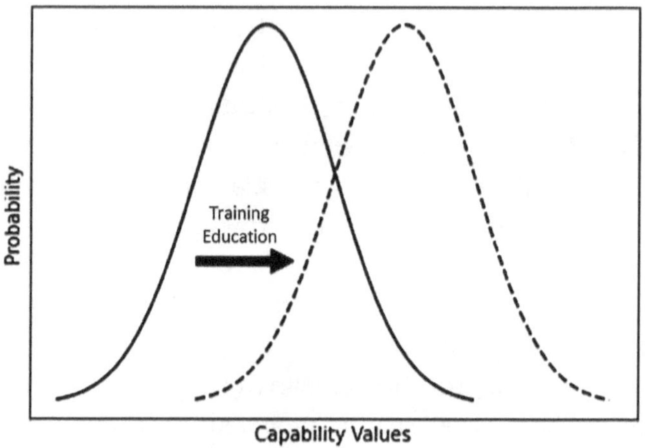

Recognizing such responses and trends may benefit the planning of education and training for individual and societies or countries. Perhaps it would be beneficial for individuals and countries to avoid indiscriminately training all equally to acquire one kind of skills, such as engineering or scientific research. After certain levels of basic education, it may be more productive for individuals to find their relative strengths, and train themselves in areas for which their performance would be above average for work and career.

Diversity and normal distribution may be two key factors to consider when considering work or career planning. People always have different strengths and weaknesses, and societies need waiters, electricians, and plumbers as well as doctors, engineers, and scientists. Their works are all essential for humanity and should be equally respected. However, it does not seem necessary to require all people, both would-be plumbers and would-be scientists, to receive equally high-level education like four-year college or graduate schools. It would be more cost- and effort-effective for individuals and societies if education and training become more selective and targeted than the widely practiced way of forcing all to try to achieve higher and higher levels of education.

While it is important to raise minimal wages so that people who do all kinds of honest works can gain a decent living, the human societies should not coerce all people to indiscriminately gain more and more education and training. Many people are studying and working harder and harder but cannot gain a good living while advanced technologies have dramatically increased productivity. Societies should plan and find better ways to distribute wealth than forcing everyone to endlessly study and work, such that life for many has become all about working and not enjoying. No matter how much education or training is imposed on young students, exceptional scientists like Einstein or great leaders like Lincoln will still be rare. Indiscriminative training and education would not change the shape of distribution of human capabilities of societies, and thus they are unlikely to positively influence the trajectory of humanity, while creating unnecessary work and stress for many people.

Notably, political and social views are influenced by multiple genetic and environmental factors and are thus likely quantitative traits. Thus, normal distribution pattern would indicate what good approaches for social governance are. For different human abilities, the standard deviation can vary. For simple skills like understanding and managing how to spend money on essential living requirements such as housing, clothing, and food, most people have a reasonably good comprehension. In these cases, the standard deviation of the distribution, σ, would be quite small. The difference between the skills of people near the average and those outside 1σ is not big. In contrast, for more sophisticated skills, such as understanding and applying math or carrying out innovative research, the standard deviation would be larger. The different between the average and those in top 0.1 percent would be huge. That is, the average person cannot apply math productively, like a mathematician can.

Therefore, one can see that when considering and deciding issues about which most of the general population have a reasonably good understanding, democracy may work well. For example, in the operation of local governments, which involves mainly collecting taxes and using taxes for tangible things such as building roads and parks and schools, strong democratic governance, such as that existing in Texas, may work very well. Whether democracy works well in a particular time and country depends on the extent to which the actual ability required for governing overlaps with voters' understanding and appreciation of politicians' characteristics. For example, in the USA voters often like those politicians who are physically attractive and are perceived to be a likable person. As such, elected leaders are often likable persons who are average in intelligence and other capabilities. In peaceful and prosperous times, such leaders can carry on with no major harm.

However, during times of major crises, a successful

leader needs to have exceptional resolve, courage, moral integrity, and high intelligence to comprehend complex situations and make wise decisions in a timely fashion. The standard deviations for all these qualities in the human population are very large. That is, the average person is very much less capable of comprehending and resolving the issues involved in crises. The successful leader would be way beyond 0.1 percent of the population, and is unlikely to be selected by average voters. In recent times in the USA, the voters have particularly been attracted to candidates' superficial styles and their narratives in the absence of substances or merits. There is a complete disconnect between the characteristics that attract voters and the characteristics that are required to successfully lead the country and the world. Under such circumstances, democracy would not work well for the country and the world as a whole. This may in part explain why, despite the tremendous advances in science and technology, the world is such a tumultuous place.

Well over 50 percent of the people, the majority in a democracy, are always concerned with their immediate wealth and life, as they should be. During recent centuries, the world has been led by Western democracies. Democracy dictates that the leaders must address the immediate interests of their voters. Thus, world events have been dictated by the immediate interests of these leading democracies. Consequently, there were two world wars fought following the industrial revolution for the world's leading democracies to divide the resources on Earth. Likewise, democracy has dictated that various governments take advantage of modern technologies to improve lives of their voters. Thus, coal and then oil and gas have been used in great quantities to improve the living standard of Western countries. This caused great deterioration in Earth's environment before developing countries like China and India even started their own industrial advance.

As democracy dictates that their government must fight in a timely fashion for their own voters' interests, Western leading countries are always fighting for their immediate interests. This continued after World Wars I and II and the Cold War. Currently, the Western leading democracies are again fighting aggressively and immediately to protect their interests in high tech against China and any other perceived hostile forces. This kind of struggle to protect immediate interests has consistently demanded convenient ignorance of moral standards. Western democracies have always chosen to stand by friendly dictators and have tolerated and encouraged highly discriminatory cultures and societies while ignoring the moral and ethical grounds of their perceived adversaries.

For example, the USA and Western countries aggressively supported the extremely corrupt government under Chiang Kai-shek against the communists in China. While retrospectively the experience of various countries has shown that communism simply does not work, the overwhelming majority of the Chinese communists were committed and driven by Confucius ideology of sacrificing and working toward a better world for all people. They were driven by noble causes, despite the numerous mistakes they made along the way. Again, the movement to crack down on corruption under President Xi is also driven by many good people whose intention is indeed noble.

In all these cases, Western countries, driven by their aggressive acts to protect their interests, real or perceived, have been dismissive of good people's noble intents and acts. Obsessed with the interests of their own voters in order to stay in power, Western leaders, exemplified by the recent presidency, often forgo any moral and ethical values. This kind of practices caused the chaos and inequality developed in many parts of the world, including Western democracies such as the USA, despite the rapid advancement of science and technology.

As a result, the condition on Earth has become very precarious, and Western leaders cannot find science-based, apolitical methods to tackle the serious threats for humanity. For example, in the USA, every piece of legislation is full of politically motivated loopholes, favors, and goodies for constituents of the left and right. The system has becoming increasingly lacking in any idea of sacrifice, but rather is all about everyone getting goodies for themselves. Consequently, the conditions for a substantial portion of the populations in Western countries, as well as the world, have been deteriorating, despite the tremendous advance of science and technology.

I certainly do not support dictatorship. However, it is worth noting that the greatest emperor of China, Li Shimin of the Tang dynasty, was well known to be able to take sharp criticisms from his subordinates. One of his trusted subordinates and a blunt critic, Wei Zhen, actually advocated the emperor's assassination when he worked under the emperor's brother. However, the idea that democracy is the preordained way of best governance is not based on history or data, but only on hyperbole and grand declarations. Democracies, exemplified by the USA, are making many poor decisions to protect their own immediate interests that are harmful to their long-term interests, Earth, or humanity as whole. One notable example may be the inflation caused by quantitative easing and the fiscal stimulus which the US federal government carried out prior to and during the COVID pandemic. Such decisions to appease voters for short-term political powers will ultimately adversely affect all humanity on Earth. This must be seriously considered by those with intelligence and good will for the common interest of humanity. Democratic elections do not automatically yield ethical and moral results, as so many democratically elected governments of the world are very abusive to women and minorities such as gays. Human ethics and morality should not be determined by democracy. Otherwise, the world shall always be ruled by powerful dark forces, thugs, war lords, and so on, as human history has so amply shown. The truth is mostly likely not to be held by masses, but by the very few wise ones. The energy of masses always needs to be guided by a strong ethical and moral force to bring about a better world. Otherwise, the energy of the masses can often lead to genocides, wars, and crusades.

Abraham Lincoln, not the masses, decided and guided the public to support the Civil War, a morally justified but brutal war. Likewise, Franklin D. Roosevelt, not the masses, decided and guided the public to fight Nazi Germany and Japan during World War II, another brutal war. Human history in the last couple hundred years is unlikely to have been the same without Lincoln and FDR. Politicians and leaders tell the public that the people are the determining force all the time, because they want to motivate and manipulate them to support their pursuit of power, as Mao Zedong of China and Donald J. Trump of USA have so masterfully shown. The power of masses, democracy, can be very deadly and immoral when manipulated by a dark force. The Western progressives should recognize this truth and the naiveté of their utopic ideas, to try to avoid extreme misfortune for their countries and humanity, as the movement of recent extreme forces in the USA should have alerted.

1. Wang T, Ashrafi A, Konduri PC, Ghosh P, Dey S, Modareszadeh P, Salamat N, Alemi PS, Berisha E, Zhang L. 2021. Heme Sequestration as an Effective Strategy for the Suppression of Tumor Growth and Progression. *Mol Cancer Ther* 20:139-49

2. Dey S, Ashrafi A, Vidal C, Jain N, Kalainayakan SP, Ghosh P, Alemi PS, Salamat N, Konduri PC, Kim JW, Zhang L. 2022. Heme Sequestration Effectively Suppresses the Development and Progression of Both Lung Adenocarcinoma and Squamous Cell Carcinoma. *Mol Cancer Res* 20:2506-18

3. Tafreshi D. 2022. Adolphe Quetelet and the legacy of the "average man" in psychology. *Hist Psychol* 25:34-55

4. Jahoda G. 2015. Quetelet and the emergence of the behavioral sciences. *Springerplus* 4: 473

5. Eknoyan G. 2008. Adolphe Quetelet (1796–1874), the average man and indices of obesity. *Nephrol Dial Transplant* 23: 47–51

6. Fisher RA. 1918. The correlation between relatives on the supposition of Mendelian inheritance. *Trans. R. Soc. Edinb* 52: 399–433

7. Deary IJ, Johnson W, Houlihan LM. 2009. Genetic foundations of human intelligence. *Hum Genet* 126: 215–32

8. Toledano-Toledano F, Moral de la Rubia J, Broche-Perez Y, Dominguez-Guedea MT, Granados-Garcia V. 2019. The

measurement scale of resilience among family caregivers of children with cancer: a psychometric evaluation. *BMC Public Health* 19: 1164

9. Primack BA, Colditz JB, Cohen E, Switzer GE, Robinson GF, Seltzer DL, Rubio DM, Kapoor WN. 2014. Measurement of social capital among clinical research trainees. *Clin Transl Sci* 7: 33–7

10. Zhou Y, Liang Y, Li K, Bai X, Chen G, Xing Z, Xiao J. 2012. The phenotypic distribution of quantitative traits in a wild mouse F1 population. *Mamm Genome* 23: 232–40

11. Jeck WR, Siebold AP, Sharpless NE. 2012. Review: a meta-analysis of GWAS and age-associated diseases. *Aging Cell* 11: 727–31

12. Chawar C, Hillmer A, Sanger S, D'Elia A, Panesar B, Guan L, Xie DX, Bansal N, Abdullah A, Kapczinski F, Pare G, Thabane L, Samaan Z. 2021. A systematic review of GWAS identified SNPs associated with outcomes of medications for opioid use disorder. *Addict Sci Clin Pract* 16: 70

13. Garfield V. 2021. Sleep duration: A review of genome-wide association studies (GWAS) in adults from 2007 to 2020. *Sleep Med Rev* 56: 101413

14. Kim KW, Ober C. 2019. Lessons Learned From GWAS of Asthma. *Allergy Asthma Immunol Res* 11: 170–87

15. Visscher PM, Wray NR, Zhang Q, Sklar P, McCarthy MI, Brown MA, Yang J. 2017. 10 Years of GWAS Discovery: Biology, Function, and Translation. *Am J Hum Genet* 101: 5–22

16. Plomin R, Haworth CM, Davis OS. 2009. Common disorders are quantitative traits. *Nat Rev Genet* 10: 872–8

17. Wang Z, Zhang Q, Lin J-R, Jabalameli MR, Mitra J, Nguyen N, Zhang ZD. 2021. Deep post-GWAS analysis identifies potential risk genes and risk variants for Alzheimer's disease, providing new insights into its disease mechanisms. *Scientific Reports* 11: 20511

18. Wang Y, Wang JG. 2018. Genome-Wide Association Studies of Hypertension and Several Other Cardiovascular Diseases. *Pulse* 6: 169–86

19. Xue A, Wu Y, Zhu Z, Zhang F, Kemper KE, Zheng Z, Yengo L, Lloyd-Jones LR, Sidorenko J, Wu Y, Agbessi M, Ahsan H, Alves I, Andiappan A, Awadalla P, Battle A, Beutner F, Bonder Marc J, Boomsma D, Christiansen M, Claringbould A, Deelen P, Esko T, Favé M-J, Franke L, Frayling T, Gharib S, Gibson G, Hemani G, Jansen R, Kähönen M, Kalnapenkis A, Kasela S, Kettunen J, Kim Y, Kirsten H, Kovacs P, Krohn K, Kronberg-Guzman J, Kukushkina V, Kutalik Z, Lee B, Lehtimäki T, Loeffler M, Marigorta UM, Metspalu A, Milani L, Müller-Nurasyid M, Nauck M, Nivard M, Penninx B, Perola M, Pervjakova N, Pierce B, Powell J, Prokisch H, Psaty B, Raitakari O, Ring S, Ripatti S, Rotzschke O, Ruëger S, Saha A, Scholz M, Schramm K, Seppälä I, Stumvoll M, Sullivan P, Teumer A, Thiery J, Tong L, Tönjes A, van Dongen J, van Meurs J, Verlouw J, Völker U, Võsa U, Yaghootkar H, Zeng B, McRae AF, Visscher PM, Zeng J, Yang J, e QC. 2018. Genome-wide association analyses identify 143 risk variants and putative regulatory mechanisms for type 2 diabetes. *Nature Communications* 9: 2941

5

INSIGHTS FROM NUCLEAR CHAIN REACTIONS

While internet and related technologies have dramatically changed the ways to work and to interact with people, the energy from nuclear reactions, as shown by nuclear bombs, is arguably still the most shocking and awesome power unleashed by modern scientific research. Einstein's theory of special relativity defined the relationship between energy and matter in this famous formula:

$$E = mc^2 \text{ or } \Delta E = \Delta mc^2.$$

E = energy; m = mass, and c = the speed of light = 2.99792×10^8 m/s.

This shows that a small amount of mass or loss of mass can be transformed into a tremendous amount of energy, because the speed of light is a very large number. During World War II, American scientists unleashed this tremendous energy by creating the atomic bomb. Scientists took advantage of the fact that certain isotopes of heavy elements, such as uranium-235 and plutonium-239, undergo fission when a neutron strikes their nucleus. When a uranium-235 atom is bombarded by a neutron, it fissions into two new atoms, releasing three neutrons and some binding energy. These neutrons in turn can fission three more uranium-235 nuclei, producing 9 neutrons, which can produce 27 neutrons in the third repetition, followed by the fourth with 81, and so on. Within a few microseconds, a very large number of nuclei fission, releasing a tremendous amount of energy and resulting in an atomic explosion.

However, some neutrons can be lost and are not available for the fission reaction. For the chain reaction to become self-sustaining, a critical mass is necessary. In an atom bomb, a mass of fissile material greater than the critical mass must be compressed together so that the atoms are close enough for the released neutrons to continue to hit, in order to generate an uncontrolled chain reaction and explosion.

Subsequently, scientists took advantage of fusion reaction to create the hydrogen bomb. Using the heat and pressure of fission, hydrogen-2 can fuse with hydrogen-3 and form helium-4 and one neutron and release energy. There is no theoretical limit to the explosive force of a fusion weapon. The world's first hydrogen bomb detonated by the USA had 700 times as great destructive force as that of the atomic bomb that destroyed Hiroshima. The largest hydrogen bomb detonated by the USSR (Union of Soviet Socialist Republics) on October 30, 1961, was 3,333 times as destructive as the atomic bomb that destroyed Hiroshima.

From nuclear reactions, we may glean some characteristics of truly transformative events that involve fundamental changes in the existence of matters. The first characteristic is that a receptive subject, such as a large, unstable atom uranium-235, must exist. The second characteristic is that a chain reaction should be initiated. The third characteristic is that extreme conditions may be created. For example, for fusion reactions to occur, extremely high pressure and temperature generated by fission reactions is necessary. Fourthly, a transformative event may release a tremendous amount of energy that fundamentally alters the world. The characteristics of a truly transformative event are multi-dimensional.

Considering the recorded human history in the past three thousand years, the events that threatened humanity as a whole have not been natural disasters, at least not directly. Rather, humanity's serious threats have always been from humans ourselves, or human-related activities. The transformative events in human history invariably involve human conflicts and epidemics aided by human activities. Those transformative events that had changed the trajectory of humanity may include crusades, Black Plague, World War I plus Spanish flu, and World War II.

Previous major events in human history, such as the French Revolution, the American Revolution, the industrial revolution, and World War I, have influenced the existence of human conditions and the development of human societies on Earth. However, until World War II, these changes in the human world were mostly one-dimensional and did not involve changes in multiple dimensions including governance, technology, and the Earth environment. Thus, the conditions for the potential upcoming transformative events are very different from the conditions that have promoted the previous transformative events in human history. Metaphorically, if we consider previous transformative events as the explosion of conventional bombs, the potential upcoming transformative events may be the explosion of nuclear bombs.

6

MAJOR THREATS TO THE FUTURE OF HUMANITY—A TRILOGY

In recorded human history, humanity has experienced thousands of years of relative homeostasis in the absence of advanced science and technology that can drastically alter the environment on Earth. However, since the industrial revolution and particularly after World War II, science and technology have greatly advanced, resulting in dramatic changes in human living conditions and enabling humanity to gain powerful tools that can produce both positive and destructive results, including strong adverse impact on the environment. Metaphorically speaking, one may say that before industrial revolution, humanity was riding leisurely on a horse carriage. When industrial revolution happened, humanity boarded a train with a diesel engine. In the new millennium, humanity is on a fast train with ever increasing speed, which is now accelerating into an unknown future— paradise, hell, or neither? To use a cliché, one's worse threat is always oneself. Humanity's great development has created major threats to its own future in the following three distinctive but related areas:

Firstly, the incredible advances in modern medicine and uninhibited reproduction of humans in many parts of the world have led to the growth of the human population from about 200 million some 2,000 years ago to 7.9 billion and growing today. The over-proliferation of humans has led to unprecedented destruction and changes in the environment. Major changes include pollution, the loss of biodiversity, and global warming. A 2014 study by the World Wildlife Fund indicated that the planet has lost 52 percent of its biodiversity since 1970. The *Living Planet Report 2014* claims, "the number of mammals, birds, reptiles, amphibians and fish across the globe is, on average, about half the size it was 40 years ago." One may imagine that all terrestrial living organisms form a pyramid, with humans on the top. With diminishing biodiversity, the base of the pyramid is shrinking. If not stopped, this will destabilize the whole structure and ultimately cause the top to crash down.

Secondly, advanced science and technology have provided tremendous tools for humans to not only improve living conditions, but also cause catastrophic destruction. Such tools include nuclear bombs, modern biotechnology, and computation power/artificial intelligence. Particularly, a neglected area of potential threats comes from the development of biotechnology. Scientists can engineer new and old pathogens, which may be spread or used as biological weapons, knowingly or unknowingly. With technology like CRISPR, scientists can also easily change the genetic makeup of various organisms, without knowing exactly what the long-term consequences will be. In their efforts to pursue fame, money, and a God-like feeling, people are rushing to create technologies and organisms that may provide some or little tangible benefits to humanity as a whole, but may harbor potential grave threats to humanity. While the exact origin of COVID-19 may not ever be determined with certainty, the tools to recreate and edit the genetic makeup of pathogens like viruses and bacteria and other living organisms have been developed and can be easily used by trained scientific personnel, as discussed earlier in chapter 3.

Another area of potential threats comes from artificial intelligence. The field of artificial intelligence is even less regulated than biotechnology. Further, the combination of biotechnology and artificial intelligence may bring tangible benefits to humans as well as potent threats to humanity. For example, advanced brain machine interfaces offer great potential in the treatment of neurological disorders including paralysis[1]. However, the same technology can be used for an array of potentially abusive applications, such as the creation of machine soldiers and spies. Such technologies may provide tools for unscrupulous individuals or enterprises to monitor and control the actions and behaviors of targeted persons, communities, and societies[2]. The current widely used apps, including Google, Facebook, and Twitter, have already provided the technology giants tremendous power and potential for abusive use of personal information with very little regulation. Various government officials lack the understanding and political will to take appropriate regulatory actions to guide the development and use of many advanced tools in biotechnology and computation/ artificial intelligence.

Thirdly, humanity lacks a unifying moral compass and shared moral values. While advanced technologies are increasingly integrating communities and countries on Earth, there is a complete lack of a moral and ethical compass that is in harmony with modern technologies and that can guide humanity to tackle the complex issues arising from increasing physical integration of the world and a rapidly changing environment due to advanced technologies. The dominant belief systems existing today originated one or two thousand years ago, when there was little science and technology. Furthermore, the dominant religions in the West are generally human-centric, with little consideration of the nonhuman world except for human consumption. Consequently, the belief systems derived from such religions are now causing irreconcilable conflicts with the reality of human society with its advanced technological tools.

For example, it may have made sense for humans to single-mindedly proliferate and take advantage of the resources on Earth with little concern for the environment and other living organisms 2,000 years ago, when the human population on Earth was only about 200 million. Now, with human population near 8 billion and other living organisms rapidly disappearing due to human activities, these belief systems encouraging unlimited proliferation of humans are not beneficial to humanity or Earth. Nonetheless, a substantial number of humans still adhere strongly to such belief systems.

Another substantial part of humans has evidently

recognized clear intellectual conflicts of modern human knowledge and experience with the ancient belief systems. This substantial part of humans and organizations turns to science, technology, or capital for its motivation and belief. However, science, technology, and capital are all ethically and morally neutral. They do not have an intrinsically attached ethical or moral compass. Scientists may feel morally motivated to relentlessly pursue their research, and technological giants feel morally empowered to develop biological and computational technologies, with little regard for their potential harm. Likewise, entrepreneurs may feel morally justified to pursue profits at all costs. Indeed, the human societies in advanced economies often idolize tech leaders, billionaires, and rich entertainers, as if they are heroes, regardless of their ethical or moral conditions.

This divergence of ideological bases underlies the political polarization that has been occurring in the USA. The dominant force on the right tries to cling to their belief based on ancient religion and their old, familiar ways of life, whereas the dominant force on the left tries to promote superficial economic and social equality without demanding individual responsibility. Neither force has a truly sound moral compass, but simply tries to gain as much for their powers and constituents as they can get away with. The middle ground is discarded completely. There is no long-term regard for the country, society, or the world. Everyone works to rip off as much perceived benefits as possible to their liking. These polarizing and irresponsible acts are further aided by advanced technologies, such as mobile communication tools, to magnify the impact of such acts on the world. Consequently, such acts can potentially create much greater adverse impact on the trajectory of humanity than ever before and pose potentially grave threats to the future of humanity.

Further exacerbating the threat is the power of capital to encourage and reward risky, creative, innovative acts in the absence of a moral compass. The reward of capitalism and a lack of moral compass have enabled many creative but morally and ethically challenged entrepreneurs, exemplified by Elizabeth Holms, who founded Theranos based on non-existing technology. The great success of Holms in raising money for her company says more about the society than Holms herself. After all, the skills Holms practiced are often encouraged and practiced not only in the business world, but also in the scholarly world, such as in research granting and paper publication. The art of storytelling for fast satisfaction has often superseded the actual hard, honest, and time-consuming work of researching and creating.

Thus, in the pursuit of money, fame, and power, politicians, entrepreneurs, and scientists have perfected the art of storytelling and spinning to acquire votes and money. Truth and facts are banished. Science and technology are used merely as tools to acquire fame, money, and power for those motivated individuals, with little regard for any adverse consequences of their behaviors or products. Consequently, more and more threats are created, as more and more technologies emerge. For example, more and more powerful weapons, including nuclear, biological, and computational, are developed to disrupt human lives and even to destroy

Earth. More and more satellites are launched to saturate Earth's atmosphere, with no regard for the harmful effects.

Further, among the community of countries, competition for dominance in economy and military has led countries to act recklessly with no regard for long-term adverse effects on the world and even on their own countries. For example, competition for economic dominance absurdly encourages already densely populated countries to reproduce more humans in order to grow their economy. Additionally, the fear of some races being taken over by other races also encourage segments of various countries to anticipate a hostile future with certain races disappearing when overpopulation is such an urgent threat to Earth and all living on Earth. Likewise, conflicts and arms races among countries are being encouraged to maximize profits and power for various countries. All these are done with no consideration for the world and environment as a whole. Humanity has completely disregarded humility and acts as if everything occurs to fit the desire of powerful individuals and countries.

The lack of a valid moral compass, coupled with advanced technologies and the insatiable appetite of individuals to acquire power and money, has created a very dangerous situation for the future of humanity and Earth. These individuals think and act as if they can control everything, and they can easily move to another planet when Earth is ruined. However, humans cannot control the universe and Earth, despite advanced technologies. While advanced technologies have changed human living conditions in the past decades, they have not necessarily improved the quality of life, but only have changed human lives, especially in advanced economies such as the USA and European countries. Ultimately, all the advanced technologies may not do much to improve the quality of human lives but only to accelerate the demise of humanity. In a perfect storm, the aforementioned three major threats may cause many series of chain reactions, which may work together to cause changes akin to the explosion of a nuclear weapon, sending humanity to misery and ultimate demise.

In analogy to the characteristics of nuclear explosions and transformative events, we may consider the characteristics of human conditions on Earth. Firstly, there are receptive populations for transformative changes. For example, in the USA, the dominant forces on both left and right are coveting dramatic changes. Secondly, conditions for chain reactions exist in many parts of the world. For example, the Arab spring caused a series of changes in many countries, leading to chaos that still exist many years later. Another example may be that the Obama presidency likely led to the Trump presidency and followed by extreme political polarization in the USA, which may continue to influence the country for many years to come and may have changed the trajectory of the USA as a country and people. Thirdly, advanced technologies, including biotechnology and artificial intelligence, may create an extreme condition, such as the COVID-19 pandemic or worse. In a perfect storm, multiple chain reactions may occur under extreme conditions, causing the release of a tremendous amount of destructive power, and ultimately leading to a transformative event with catastrophic consequences for humanity.

1. Musk E, Neuralink. 2019. An Integrated Brain-Machine Interface Platform with Thousands of Channels. *J Med Internet Res* 21: e16194
2. Maynard AD, Scragg M. 2019. The Ethical and Responsible Development and Application of Advanced Brain Machine Interfaces. *J Med Internet Res* 21: e16321

7

THE FUTURE OF HUMANITY: WHAT LIES AHEAD, AND WHAT CAN WE DO NOW?

Like the progression of the COVID-19 pandemic and California wildfires, many events in the human world are still very much unpredictable, despite human's advanced technologies. Furthermore, because technologies do not come with an ethical or moral compass and are often double-edge swords, they can bring about unpredictable, unforeseeable events that may dramatically impact the trajectory of humanity, as discussed in chapter 6. How can humanity better apply technologies to improve instead of dampen the future?

In essence, the three major threats discussed in chapter 6 are all related to the conflict between advanced technologies and the lack of a moral and ethical compass that is compatible with advanced technologies and can guide human applications of powerful technologies. At many levels, ranging from family and community to countries, advanced technologies have sped up and intensified the struggle between different forces, which is particularly evident in a multi-cultural country like the USA. For example, with globalization and various quick transportation machines, a highly infectious virus like COVID-19 can spread across the globe very quickly. Likewise, with powerful mobile communications tools information, fake or real, spreads very quickly to influence the actions of many people. These advanced technologies can cause quick chain reactions, which are much harder for governments to manage compared to previous times, such as during World War II.

The human experiences, particularly those in recent times, have clearly shown that simple wishes cannot change the outcome of major events that may change the trajectory of humanity. What can humanity do to better manage rapidly occurring events accelerated by advanced technologies, in order to avoid the occurrence of catastrophic events that threat the existence and well-being of humanity? To answer this question, we may first consider what has consistently worked for humanity. What has consistently worked for humanity has been the discovery and application of scientific truths and principles. The scientific truths and principles have enabled humanity to discover and utilize modern medicines to dramatically increase human health and life span; to build high-rise buildings, long bridges that cross oceans, and under-water tunnels that connect islands; to make airplanes and rockets that can fly thousands of miles; to make nuclear bombs and power generators; to build computers that can calculate much faster than the human brains; and so on.

By examining the scientific principles of the natural world, we may glean some characteristics of the human world that should promote our survival and development. Firstly, as discussed in chapters 1, 2, and 4, it can be inferred that certain scientific principles, regardless how they were initially discovered, may be applied to understand and predict the behaviors of large or small, and living or nonliving, objects. For example, the normal distribution represents not only the distribution of the errors of measurements in astronomical observations but also the distribution of human traits. In the same vein, the laws of thermodynamics may not only describe and predict the behaviors and interactions of molecules, but also those of humans.

Secondly, it is worth noting that materials discussed in chapter 3 indicate that the human world, like the natural world of all living organisms, should be diverse. Diversity benefits the survival and development of all living organisms, including humans. The normal distribution provides an approximation of the pattern and scope of diversity. Diversity exists in the living world as well as in the world of chemical bonding and molecular interactions. Diversity should occur at many levels, including diversity in individual traits (ranging from heights and weights to IQ scores and other capabilities), diversity in communities, and diversity in countries.

Third, adaptation and evolution are intrinsic to living cells and organisms in response to changes in the environment. Adaptation of a living species like *Homo sapiens* is embedded in its diversity in the form of genetic variations, as materials discussed in chapter 3 indicate. Fourth, ethics, morality, and laws are unique to human society; physical machines and technologies do not have intrinsic ethical or moral characteristics. Thus, advanced science and technologies do not ensure a morally sound development. For example, Nazi Germany could efficiently develop and apply technologies like any other country. *Humans alone must take the responsibility in ethics and morality.*

Having a universal moral and ethical principle is not only possible, but also rational and necessary for humanity to thrive. In the case of the natural physical and living world, there is tremendous diversity existing on Earth while all matters, living or nonliving, conform to the universal laws and principles of physics, chemistry, and mathematics. The living world also conforms to the principles of genetics and other biological principles. Likewise, the human world can have a universal moral and ethical compass while having great diversity in individuals, communities, and countries.

For sustainable development of a population, culture, or country, the moral and ethical principles should not conflict with scientific principles that govern physical and life sciences. This should be the *first criterion* of a universal moral compass: The moral codes or compass of humanity should be in harmony with scientific laws of physical and life sciences. In discussing morality, God/almighty often comes up. If we accept that God is universally powerful, then we must also recognize that science and technology, no matter how powerful, must also be under God's purview. In other words, science and technology are just one domain under God's governance. No matter how much scientific knowledge and technology humanity acquires, all of them must be under God's governance. Thus, science and technology do not conflict with the existence and acceptance of God. It is logically difficult to rationalize that a universally powerful God does not govern science and technology. In other words, the human world, along with all the knowledge and technologies known to humanity, likely represents a small part of the God's universe. Thus, whatever is scientific does not counter God, and whatever is counter-scientific must not be godly.

As discussed in previous chapters, the godly physical and living world is extremely diverse. Thus, sustaining and promoting diversity of the natural and human worlds must be the *second criterion* of a universal moral compass. Humanity's actions should always promote diversity at multiple levels—at the levels of species, human individuals, communities, cultures, and countries. Furthermore, humanity is the most capable of all living organisms existing on the godly Earth. As the most powerful organism, humanity should not abuse its power and feel entitled to exhaust Earth's resources. This is not beneficial to humanity itself and very damaging to other God-endowed living organisms. Humanity's unrelenting proliferation has been disastrous for the survival of many living organisms, including numerous mammals. As the most powerful living being on Earth, humanity should take responsibility to protect Earth and promote the long-term survival and development of all living organisms. Humanity should take direct responsibility and not blame machines which it has created. The responsibilities should be taken at multiple levels—at the levels of individuals, communities, and countries. Thus, the *third criterion* of a universal moral compass should be taking responsibilities.

As many individuals, communities, and governments have recognized, humanity faces grave challenges in the destruction of Earth's resources and environment. Under such perilous conditions, to ensure the long-term survival and development of humanity and other godly creatures on Earth, it is of utmost importance that humanity seeks truths and facts in order to save the world. While wonderful wishes and fantastic expressions can be very pleasing, they will not solve the serious problems—the ever-increasing occurrences of natural disasters, the conflicts among countries and cultures, the destruction of the natural environment, and the creation and control of dangerous high-tech weapons, including nuclear, biological, and computational weapons (e.g., hackers or artificial intelligence tools). Humanity has created these powerful tools that can destroy Earth many times, in the absence of natural disasters. If humanity refuses to recognize these dangers and respond seriously, in a perfect storm of human and natural incidents, a condition for the ultimate demise of humanity can be created. Thus, the *fourth criterion* of a universal moral compass must be to recognize and seek truths and to be honest with each other in order to save humanity from self-destruction.

To sum up, a moral compass shared by all humans, religious, spiritual, or atheistic, should be as follows: *respect scientific principles of physical and life sciences, promote diversity at all levels, take responsibility for actions and consequences, and seek truth and honesty.* With such a universal moral compass guiding the practice of humanity, or at least those in the dominant parts of the world, the current perilous situation of the world would gradually dissipate, and humanity's survival and development are likely to continue.

With a universal moral compass, we may then proceed to lessen the major threats facing humanity. The first major threat is that caused by increasing human populations. The unlimited human proliferation in recent decades on Earth has enabled humanity to outcompete virtually all other living species on Earth for resources, fundamentally altering Earth's environment and causing the extinction of many living species. This in turn pose serious threats to humanity. Furthermore, increasing human populations are causing more and more competitions among communities and countries. In order to gain advantages in economic and military competitions among different countries and races, governments and business leaders perversely encourage uninhibited proliferation of human populations in all countries. The actions of political and business leaders are guided by short-term interests and encourage lose-lose competitions among countries and races.

Instead of facing the real issue that threatens Earth—the ever-increasing human populations—political and business leaders try to find superficial solutions for short-term profits. While any attempts to conserve energy and resources are beneficial and should be encouraged, leaders need to be serious about the real solutions to the problems. For example, with billions of people on Earth all trying to improve their lives by having machines such as air conditioners and vehicles which consume energy, and with various regions still needing to use high-pollution energy sources such as coal to general energy, the use of electric vehicles would not appear to be an effective solution for the serious problem of pollution on Earth. The use of electric vehicles can reduce pollution in selected areas, such as those countries with an advanced economy. However, the use of coal and other dirty energy sources in a substantial number of less advanced countries would still cause increased pollution.

Increased populations will not only cause pollution by using more energy, but also by many other means, including generating more wastes as well as needing more houses, food, and so on. As the less advanced economies improve their living standards, the increasing threat to the environment has no end. Thus, it is critical for all leaders—political, business, and religious—to recognize that the real threat facing humanity is humanity itself. Humanity needs to take responsibility for its own actions, not to blame mere machines, to do the right thing for the love of other God-endowed living organisms on Earth, for Earth, and for God, if one may say.

Another important way to lessen the major threats is to accept and act in accordance with truth, honesty, and facts. With improved living conditions brought about by advanced science, medicine, and technologies, humans have increasingly chosen to tackle various issues with the feel-good approach, often regardless of truth and facts. The approach of spinning the issues is not only frequently practiced in politics, but also in business and even in scientific research for the sake of seeking grant funding and flashy publications. Consequently, there is little trust among different segments of the society. The COVID-19 pandemic has exposed this worldwide lack of trust of governments and scientists.

Humanity needs to not fear truth and honesty. Humans have dramatically improved their lives based on scientific truths. With truth, humans are empowered to make great impact. Likewise, accepting truths in all aspects of human society should only empower humans to do better in all aspects of life. Problems may appear superficially to be resolved using hypocritical, feel-good solutions in the near term. However, such solutions not only do not solve any problems, but also serve to exacerbate the problems. For example, it is not clear how affirmative action serves any long-term goal in reaching equality, but it often serves to inhibit real equality due to suspicions and resentments that it engenders. Humanity should not fear truths, but only untruths presented as truths by unscrupulous politicians, businessmen, and scientists for their personal gains. With truth and honesty, humanity can lessen the threats by better regulating powerful technologies, including nuclear, biological, and computational technologies. Truth and honesty will also lesson the conflicts between different religious beliefs, cultures, and countries.

Another important factor is diversity. Diversity is amply observed in physical and living environments. Diversity is beneficial at all levels of the human world. The Western liberal democracies often encourage diversity in the local living and work environment. However, their lack of acceptance of diversity in other key areas, such as ideology and governing approaches, serves to inhibit greater diversity in the world. For example, the dominating forces in left and right are increasingly unable to accept and work with people with different ideologies.

The Western democracies also universally claim that the majority-rule democracy is the best way of governing. However, this is merely based on hyperbole and wishful thinking. As the normal curve demonstrates, the vast majority of the population are located in the middle of the curve with representative but ordinary levels of human capabilities or traits. Particularly in areas such as international relations, very few people in many countries have any real comprehension of such complex things. Likewise, the vast majority of people lack the capabilities to rapidly respond to crisis, such as COVID-19 infections or a war. In these cases where the representative majority have a virtually complete lack of understanding, democracy does not yield acceptable results. In other words, scientifically, democracy would only yield good results when dealing with issues on which that the vast majority of the people have a good understanding. It is hard to imagine the allies would have won World War II if the political leaders in the USA and Britain had acted in the way the current leaders of Western democracies often do—to follow polls. In crisis when only highly capable individuals can make the right decisions, democracy does not serve to yield good results.

Clearly, while the leaders in the Western world promote diversity in certain areas, they are unable to accept and promote diversity in thinking and governing. This can cause great sufferings in the people of the world, such as the sufferings experienced by people in the Middle East during recent decades. This lack of acceptance of diversity in ideas is also destabilizing the American society. The practice of moral communism, exemplified by affirmative action and political correctness, does not work, in the same way that material communism did not work, which was demonstrated convincingly by the failed practices of communism in Eastern Europe and China. Nowadays, the Chinese Communist Party is really practicing economic compassionate conservatism.

Importantly, humanity needs to recognize and accept that democracy is only a governing method, not the ultimate goal. Humanity's goal should be the pursuit of freedom, equality, and justice. Whatever governance method can enable people to succeed in this goal should be accepted, and humanity should not stop to search the best way of governance. It is worth pointing out that while equality and justice can be more or less defined straightforwardly, the practice of seeking freedom is less straightforward. Humans need to pursue freedom with a clear understanding and respect of others' freedom and with respect for equality and justice. The environmental problem on Earth is largely caused by humanity's pursuit of freedom with superior tools that enable humanity to outcompete all other living species and eventually become its own worst enemy.

Clearly, humanity has achieved tremendous success on Earth. As a result, humans have no more dangerous species than humanity itself on Earth. In the same vein, humanity poses the greatest threat to their homeland, Earth. Recent events have revealed ample telltale signs of the disastrous consequences of humanity's unchecked power in proliferation, application of advanced technologies, and lose-lose competitions. It is a critical time for responsible political, business, and thought leaders to take a long-term view of where humanity is going and to examine the potentially long-term, grave consequences of powerful technologies and weaponries before rushing to develop them.

It is lucky for humanity that none of the huge number of nuclear weapons developed during the Cold War by the USSR and USA has been actually deployed. However, will humanity continue to be so lucky with all other technologies and weaponries? Maybe not. Perhaps the COVID-19 pandemic should serve as a strong warning to humanity: Humanity has the power to create destructive agents, including synthetic viruses, pathogens, and nuclear weapons, but humanity may not have control over them once they are deployed. Chain reactions can happen, and a perfect storm can materialize to bring humanity to its knees or complete destruction. It is the time for humanity to gain some humility and really accept that the power of God belongs to God alone, and no humans should be so arrogant to act godly, to bring about God's severe lessons.